Do Your Own Company Administration

By Sadick Keshavjee

Trafford rev. 10/21/2016

 www.trafford.com

North America & international
toll-free: 1 888 232 4444 (USA & Canada)
fax: 812 355 4082

PREFACE

In most commonwealth or common law countries corporate law has evolved from England. So this booklet whilst it explains matters in general terms does so on the basis of such 'received' law. The first major, substantive company law legislation was Cap 486 which has been referred to throughout the book. Each country including the UK has enacted legislation to suit evolving conditions pertaining to its own jurisdiction. But the concepts and principles generally do apply.

This is a do it yourself manual for all persons ranging from one who is contemplating doing business, by incorporating a company, or one working in a large corporation-even listed, that has a corporate secretarial department.

This booklet has been created for informational purposes only and is not a substitute for legal advice.

There is no doubt that knowledge is power and education is invaluable. Whilst the training offered is obviously not a substitute for legal advice. Everyone's legal issue is unique.

Legalshield is the best next step

The mission statement of Legal Shield;

'Our vision is to provide access to the Liberty, Equality, Opportunity, and Justice that every North American deserves and expects'

With the commitment of over 4 million LegalShield members, at the time of writing, they are able to negotiate comprehensive legal services with dedicated law firms in several states in USA and provinces in Canada, at a fraction of what they traditionally cost. (Uncommonly accessible legal services at an uncommonly affordable price.)

They are listed on the New York Stock Exchange.

You get a dedicated law firm you can count on when you need legal advice.

Just contact legalshield.com and quote the founders name (Sadick Keshavjee associate no. 701521). Membership will facilitate a 50 pc discount coupon for one of our courses.(Limited period -and first come first served) .This website gives a general overview of legal plan coverage, and which North American State (USA) or Province (Canada).

CONTENTS

COMPANY ADMINISTRATION FOR NOVICES

ABOUT THE BOOK

Whether one wants to incorporate a business or work as a corporate administrator this book will give an in -depth look at various aspects of such an undertaking.

The author first covers all aspects of meetings like notice requirements, agendas, resolutions and minutes of meetings.

The next chapter covers rights and obligations of directors of companies.

The author then covers the subject of shares, registers of members transfer and transmission of shares and then forfeiture.

There is a chapter of borrowing powers of directors.

Then follows a discussion on the increase and decrease of share capital.

Finally the author discusses company books and accounts and general duties of auditors.

The book then goes on to discuss the memorandum and articles of association (constitution) of the company, followed by different types of possible clauses.

What follows is a questionnaire that one would have to complete, to start the ball rolling on setting up a company.

The Source of Corporate law is the UK for most commonwealth countries "When the sun never set in the British Empire".

I have thus used the basis of this booklet on the companies' act of UK of 1948. This was the first hall mark pieces of legislation which formed the basis on which future legislation expanded upon the UK and other commonwealth countries.

ABOUT THE AUTHOR

The author had studied law with the University of London, with company law as one of his options after becoming a full member of the Institute of Chartered Secretaries and administrators after passing all their exams.

Not only has he has practical experience in the field of corporate trusteeship, in a Canadian Trust company but has written several articles, a procedure manual for an international consulting firm in the field.

I

Company Administration

Kinds of Registered Companies

The kind of company that will be considered in this work is the company limited by shares. Other kinds of companies are-

- Companies limited by guarantee, with or without a capital divided into shares
- Unlimited companies

Companies limited by Shares

They are associations of persons (except in the case of "Private" companies – hereinafter defined) for the promotion of some lawful object (generally for the purposes of profit), possessing a common capital contributed to by each other member, the capital being divided into shares. The main feature is limited liability. That is, the liability of each member is limited to the amount unpaid of the nominal value of the share or shares he agrees to take.

Joint stock companies are promoted for reasons other than that of obtaining limited liability. Undertaking requiring a large capital can scarcely be promoted without participation and financial support of very many individuals, yet, on the other hand the law forbids any business to be carried on by a "company, association, or partnership" if its membership exceeds twenty or if the business be banking if the members exceed ten unless the association is registered as a company incorporation is thus forced upon associations requiring to approach the public for the subscription of large amounts of capital but the benefits of incorporation are such that advantage is taken where a partner in a business he has a better opportunity of doing so if the business be converted into one having a capital divided into shares with limited liability, and in practice many businesses are converted in order the more easily to obtain the necessary working capital to replace that which has been taken from the business by the withdrawal of a partner.

A company is a corporate body, capable of suing and of being sued in its corporate capacity and is a quite distinct and separate being in the eyes of the law from the persons who comprise its membership, even though one person may hold practically all the shares and personally conduct the business.

"Private" Companies

A private company is one which restricts the right to transfer its shares; and limits the number of its members not including persons who are in the employment of the company and persons who, having been formerly in employment of the company, where,while in the employment. And have continued after the determination of that employment to be, members of the company; and prohibits any invitation to the public to subscribe.

Where two or more persons hold a share or shares jointly they are treated as a single member, If a private company so after its articles that they no longer include the necessary provisions for a private company, the company ceases to be a private company musty within fourteen days of the alteration, file with the register a prospectus or statement in lieu.

If the company, whilst not altering its articles, fails to comply with the provisions which constitute it a private company then unless that court is satisfied that the failure was accidental the company will no longer be entitled to trade with less than seven members.

There is no exemption for an ordinary private company from circulating to its members it annual balance sheet and auditors and directors report at least twenty one days before the annual general meeting.

Documents to be filed upon Incorporation

Companies are incorporated by filling with the registrar of companies, the following documents-

1. Memorandum of Association.
2. Articles of Association (if any).

3. Statement of nominal capital.
4. Statutory declaration of compliance with the companies act and in the case of public companies.
5. List of persons who have consented to be directors.
6. Their forms of consent to act as directors of the company.
7. Their contracts to take their qualification shares, unless they have signed the memorandum for a sufficient number.

Wherever possible, it is also advisable to file with these documents, the notice of the situation of the registered office and a copy of the register of directors and secretaries.

Memorandum of Association

He memorandum is a document which by sect 5 of the companies act must contain in the case of a company limited by shares:-

1. The name of the company, with "limited" as the last word in its name;
2. The country where the registered office is to be situated.
3. The objects for which the company is established.
4. A declaration that the liability of the members is limited.
5. The amount of the share capital with which the company proposes to be registered and how such share capital is to be divided (the shares fixed amounts) subject to
   a) Each subscriber to the memorandum taking (at least one share)
   b) Each subscriber writing opposite his name the number of shares he agrees to take.

Seven subscribers are required to a memorandum in the case of a public company, only two being necessary for a private company.

The memorandum requires careful drafting. No company may be registered with a name which is undesirable.

The following notes regarding names are given by the register of companies for the guidance of the public, though it must be understood that they are in no way exhaustive.

1. A name will not be allowed if it is misleading; for
2. Names cannot ordinals be allowed if they suggest coaction with a government department or any municipality or other local authority of any society or body incorporated by statue.

3. Names must not include the word "Co- Operative" or the words "Building Society"
4. Names including the following words will be allowed only where the circumstances justify it – "banking" "investment" "trust".
5. Names which include a proper name which is not the surname of the proprietors or of a director will not be allowed except for valid reasons.
6. If the proposed name includes a registered traded mark, the constant of the owner of the trade mark should be produced to the registrar of companies.
7. A name will be refused if it is too like the name of an existing company.

The Articles of Association

While the memorandum defines the name constitution and objects of the company the articles comprise its internal regulations whereby the relations between the shareholders and the company and between the directors and the company are governed in them will be found the rights of the various classes of shareholders as to dividends and voting, and as to repayment of their capital in the event of the dealt with in the memorandum instead); and how they may transfer their shares; the extent to which the management of the business is entrusted to the directors and particularly the extent to which they may borrow money on behalf of the company; the rules for the holding of meeting of members called general meetings and meetings of directors and what notice is to be given of such meetings.

The articles have to be signed by the same persons as signed the Memorandum, and witnessed.

Table, applicable to every company limited by shares for public and part II for private companies. Its clauses automatically become part of the company's own articles unless the latter definitely exclude them or modify them by providing alternative provisions

How Incorporation is Effected

The Memorandum may be printed or written, whilst the Articles must be printed; but as copies of both documents are required from time to time it is usual to have them printed and bound together in the form of a foolscap booklet. For the purposes of the formation, the printers are asked to supply copies with blanks where the signatures and descriptions, etc., of the subscribers and witness will appear; and one such copy, properly completed, is lodged with the registrar. After incorporation, the names etc. are filled in and the printers asked to supply the remaining copies completed in this manner. Printed forms for the other documents required to be registered are obtainable from law stationers. After all have been completed and signed who is attending to the registration of the company attends before a commissioner for oaths and makes the statutory declaration then deposits all the documents at the registry for inspection.

Later he will attend again at the Registry and will be informed whether the documents are in order. If they are not it may be necessary to make the necessary alterations and get then initiated by each signatory. But if the documents are in order he will be required to pay the necessary stamp duties and fees.

After the official receipt for the payment of these amounts is produced, the Certificate of Incorporation is handed over.

Publication of Name

Companies act requires a company to have its name painted or affixed on the outside of every office or place in which its business is carried on, in a conspicuous position, and in letters easily and always legible; and in all business letters, notices and other official publications of the company and in all bills of exchange promissory notes, endorsements, cheques orders for money or goods purporting to be signed by or on behalf of the company and in all bills of parcels invoices, receipts and letters of credit of the company its name shall be mentioned in legible characters. Non compliance with the requirements as to the name being affixed or painted on in every office or business place involves a penalty on the company and on every officer of the company who is in default. If compliance is not made with the requirements as to the name on the various documents above enumerated, a penalty attached to the company and to and director or manager or officer f the company who issues or authorizes the personally liable to the holder of any such bill of exchange promissory note cheque or order for money or goods in respect of the amount thereof unless it is paid by the company.

Each company must have its name engraven in legible characters on its seal, if the company fails to comply with this it is liable to a fine and any officer who uses a seal not properly engraven is liable to the same fine.

Certificate of Incorporation

Certificate shall be conclusive evidence that all the requirements of this act is in respect of registration and of matters precedent and incidental thereto have been complied with and that the association is a company authorized to be registered and duly registered under this act.

First Board Meeting

As soon as possible after the receipt of the Certificate of incorporation a meeting will be help of the persons who is intended shall be the first directors and the issue of the certificates is reported to them if as is usual they have been described by name in the articles as the first directors of the company this will be sufficient appointment but if not then it will be necessary for the subscribers who at this point are the only members of the company to appoint them either in writing signed by all of them or by meeting and passing a resolution

The directors will then proceed to do all necessary acts to set the company going they will appoint the secretary and fix his remuneration they will authorize the acquisition or leasing of offices and instruct the secretary to file the address of the registered office they will adopt a design for the common seal and authorize the secretary to obtain the requisite books and stationary and engage the necessary staff and If the company has been formed to take over an existing business they will consider the execution of the purchase agreement. They will appoint bankers for this purpose the secretary will have obtained from the bankers two copies of their usual form of appointment one of which will have completed by the chairman and signed by all persons authorized to operate the account this he will later hand to bankers they will also ask to see the certificate of incorporation.

Commencement of Business

A private company assuming that this has the requisite capital may now commence business,

In the case of a company which is inviting the public to subscribe to its capital this certificate will not be issued unless,

1. The public has subscribed sufficient capital to cover the minimum subscription an amount stated by the directors in the prospectus issued to the public to be required to provide for the purchases of any property payment of preliminary expenses and the provision of the necessary working capitals;
2. The shares have actually been allotted;
3. The directors have paid on their shares the same proportion as the public have been required to pay an application as an allotment; and

4. No more money is due to applicants in respects of any shares or debentures offered for public subscription by reason of failure to apply for or to obtain permission for the shares of debentures to be dealt in on any stock exchange. A statutory declaration that these conditions have been complied with must be delivered to the Registrar by the secretary or one of the directors.

The capital of a Company

As has been stated the capital, the capital of the type of company now being considered is divided into shares. Shares are mainly of two classes ordinary and preference ordinary shares from the staple capital of a company and rank after preference shares for purposes of dividend and if the articles provide in regard to capital in a winding up. They con statute the "equity".

The preference dividend is a fixed one and is invariably cumulative unless the articles provide otherwise that is if a dividend has not been paid in respect of such shares one year arrears of dividend must be paid and soon as the company in a position to pay such arrears before the ordinary shareholders receive any dividend. Redeemable preference shares may be issued if the articles so authorize such shares to be redeemable either out of profits available for dividend or form the proceeds of a fresh issue of shares. The value of the provision lies in the fact that if interest rates generally have fallen since the issue of the preference shares and replaces them by others carrying a lower rate of dividend.

Shares may be issued at a discount provided the requirements of companies act are compiled with these include the obtaining of the sanction of the court. They must be of class already issued, be authorized at a general meeting and be issued a year or more after the company was entitled to commence business.

Where a company issues shares at a premium all sums received as premium account the amount of the share premium account mist be applied to paying up unissued shares of the company to be issued to members as fully paid bonus shares.

The following terms are used in connection with the capital of a company;

NOMINAL CAPITAL, which is the amount of capital authorized by the memorandum of association.

SUBSCRIBED CAPITAL: that is portion of the issued capital for which payment has been made.

CALLED - UP CAPITAL. The amount called up on the shares issued.

PAID –UP CAPITAL, which is the total amount paid up on shares or considered paid up.

Underwriting

Unless a company receives from its first offer of shares to the public enough applications to cover the minimum subscription it is not allowed to proceed to allot the shares or to commence business. In practice, the risk of an inadequate public response is almost invariably removed by having the issue underwritten this is effected by getting underwriters to contract, for commission on the whole issue to take up any part of it not applied for by the public or other interested party. Sometimes the underwriters will stipulate that a certain number of shares are allotted to them firm they then in effect get such shares at a discount the underwriters frequently re insure the risk they have undertaken by getting other persons to sub underwrite either the whole or a portion of the risk for commission slightly less than that which is left to the underwriters is then known as overriding commission.

The Prospectus

Prospectus any prospectus notice circular advertisement or other invitation offering to public for subscription or purchase any shares or debentures of a company the drafting of the prospectus is usually left to specialists but in any case final proofs should be passed by an advocate to ensure that all legal requirements have been complied with.

The following is a brief list of the matters required to be

1. Capital directors share qualification and remuneration;
2. Names, descriptions and addresses of the directors.
3. Minimum subscription necessary to provide the amount required to cover the purchase price of the property which is the defrayed out of the issue the preliminary expenses the amount necessary to repay and loans obtained to meet these costs and working capital;
4. The time of opening of the subscription lists;

5. Amount payable on application and allotment with particulars of previous issues, if any;

6. Number, description and amount of any shares or debentures for which any person has an option to subscribe;

7. Number and amount of shares and debentures which within the two preceding years have been issued as fully or partly paid up otherwise than in cash;

8. Names and addresses of vendors of any property to be paid out of the proceeds or the issue;

9. Amount of purchase money for such property;

10. Particulars of any underwriting commission;

11. Amount or estimate of the preliminary expenses and expenses of the issue and the persons by whom they have been paid or payable;

12. Amount paid or payable to any promoter;

13. dates of parties to and general nature of over material contract;

14. Names and addresses of auditors;

15. Particulars of any director's interest in property proposed to be acquired;

16. right of voting conferred by different classes of shares;

17. Length of time during which business has been carried on if less than three years.

These requirements are set out in full in the Third schedule and sect 40 to the companies act cap 486. If any of the proceeds of the issue are for the purchase of a business and accountants report upon the business in respect of the five previous years is to be set out. If the company has been in existence before its prospectus is issued that document must set out a report by the auditors on previous financial results for five years.

An examination of a prospectus will reveal the fact that is can be divided into three parts, viz.:

a) The legal requirements,
b) General information concerning the business or intended business, and
c) Advertisement.

The tendency of these provisions is to compel company promoters to disclose as much as possible of what is material and important for the would be investor. A good plan in studying the nature and form of a prospectus is to take one and dissect it into its several parts as above mentioned carefully nothing that all requirements of the law are complied with. A point to notice on every prospectus is that "the Prospectus has been delivered for registration to the Registrar of companies." Copy of every prospectus signed by every person names therein as a director or proposed director, to be delivered for registration on or before the day it is published and it must not be issued until this has been done. It may be noted however that many people receive what are termed advanced prospectuses, marked private before the prospectus proper has been filed and issued. The object of this is

1. To give to certain persons an opportunity to subscribe in preference to others;
2. To invite offers for underwriting; and
3. To test the feeling in regard to the prospects of the proposed company among certain number of likely investors and provided the issue is carefully restricted so that it cannot be constructed as publication to any person as a member of the public, the document will not legally be prospectus.

Directors and others responsible for the issue of a prospectus incur liability in the event of non compliance with contravention of any of the requirements of the Companies Act, unless they can show

a) That as regards any matter not disclosed they were a cognizant thereof
b) That the non compliance or contravention arose from an honest mistake of act, or
c) That it was in respect or matters which in the opinion of the court were immaterial or which ought to be excused.

The persons responsible for any misstatements in a prospectus in addition into any criminal liability may incur civil liability to pay compensation to anyone who subscribes for shares or debentures on the faith of such misstatements for any loss or damage sustained a statement in a prospectus will be considered as untrue if it is misleading in the form and context in which it is included.

The following are the persons who may be liable for misstatements

a) The directors at the time of issue of the prospectus.
b) Any person who has authorized the appearance of his name as a director or proposed director either at that or a future time.
c) Any promoter of a company other than persons acting merly in a professional capacity for persons engaged in the formation of the company.
d) All persons who have authorized the issue of the prospectus.

Offers for Sale

Any document by which an offer for sale to the public is made of shares or debentures is to be deemed for all purposes to be a prospectus issued by a company, that company allotted or agreed to allot the same with a view to their being so agreed to allot the same with a view to their being so offered for sale but without prejudice to the liability of the offertory in respect of the offer. Unless the contract is proved such allotments are to be deemed to have been made with a view to the shares or debentures being offered for sale to the public if it is shown-

a) That an offer for sale was made within six months after allotment or agreement to allot; or

b) That at the date when the offer was made the whole consideration receivable by the company in respect of the shares or debentures had not been so received.

Further such offers must also contain in addition to the particulars required to be stated in a prospectus details as to the consideration received by the company in respect of the shares or debentures in question, and particulars as to the place and time at which the contract relating thereto may be inspected.

Signatories' Shares

Generally speaking a contract to make shares in a company consists of an offer in the form an application to take the shares an acceptance of the offer by a resolution allotting the shares the acceptance being sent to the offertory in the form a letter of allotment in this case of the signatories to the Memorandum a formal allotment is sometimes made to them of the shares they have agreed to take but in some instances no such formal allotment is made in this event the signatories are deemed to have agreed to become members of the company and on its registration are to be entered as members of the company and its register of members further as they are members of the company and have indicated the number of shares they wish to take they are of course liable to pay for them.

Notice of Situation of Registered Office

This is a form that must be lodged with the Registrar within fourteen days after incorporation of the company.

We have mentioned that all companies are required to state the Memorandum of Association the situation of the office ("the domicile") within that domicile there must be a registered office. Any change in address must be notified to the Registrar within fourteen days.

II

SOME CONSIDERATION OF MEETINGS IN GENERAL

What is a Meeting?

Each companies articles require many matters to be carried out by resolution passed at a meeting it is frequently vital to know whether a meeting in the strict legal sense has been held a meeting has been defined as a coming together for a common lawful object of two or more persons; and only in very exceptional circumstances as for example where all the shares of a class are held by one member or where the rules permit the appointment of a committee of one can a single person constitute a meeting. The general rule is that a single shareholder cannot form a meeting even if he has been appointed by all the other shareholders to represent them.

For a meeting of a constituted body such as a company to be valid, it must be:

a) Properly convened;
b) Properly constituted- with the right person in the chair and quorum present;
c) Held in accordance in any applicable statutes and rules.

Quorum

A quorum is the minimum number of members who must be present before a meeting can validly transact business in the absence of any regulations at all two members are sufficient;

but in companies the articles usually make provision and where they do not the companies act prescribes a minimum of three members for general meetings of a public company and two members for a private company.

The mere physical presence of a quorum without an intention to meet does not constitute of meeting.

Notice

Except where all the members of a body are present and all agree to waive notice a meeting can be held only if proper notice has been given the principal rules relating to notice are as follows:

1. Notice must be given to all those entitled to attend but rules frequently provide that accidental omission to give notice to a member shall not in validate the proceedings.
2. Notice must state the date, time and place of meeting all of which must be reasonably convenient.
3. Notice must be issued under proper authority
4. Notice must be served I n the manner provided e.g. by post
5. The proper length of notice must be given; and unless otherwise stated, clear days notice i.e. exclusive of the day of service and of the day of the meeting, must be given.
6. The notice must state fairly and frankly the nature of business to be transacted.

Chairman

The regulations usually provide who shall be chairman. Where they do not or the chairman is not present the meeting may elect one of their numbers. By so doing there devolves on him by agreement the conduct of the meeting subject to the applicable regulations.

A chairman should be impartial, well- informed with regard to procedure, courteous, good humored and fair but firm. He must in the first place see that the meeting has been properly convened and that it is duly constituted that his own appointment is in order and a quorum present; and he must preserve order and conduct the meeting regularly and se that the sense of the meeting is properly obtained on any question placed before it.

He must give all an equal opportunity to speak so far as time permits but when a matter has been adequately discussed he may close the discussion and put the motion to the vote.

He must see that all business is within the scope of notice and must not allow irrelevant discussion or improper language. It is his duty to decide who shall speak, to put motions and amendments to vote and to declare the result if the regulations provide he has an additional or casting vote to be used only on an equality of votes to secure a decision.

A chairman should deal with points of order as they are raised.

The members have placed the control of themselves as individuals in his hands, and he is entitled to eject or have ejected any persons whose disorderly conduct prevents the transaction of business and who refuse to leave. (This power is to be exercised with due care, and the wishes of the meeting should be ascertained.) He is entitled to adjourn the meeting if necessary to preserve order, though here again the support of the majority present should be obtained.

Order on Debate

Companies (unlike legislative assemblies such as parliament) do not generally formulate standing orders to govern the conduct of their meetings, but they nevertheless observe certain rules based on custom. Thus the business should be taking order of the agenda unless the chairman varies the order in the constant of the meeting speakers stand when speaking except at the board and committee meetings and address the chair and must resume their seats if the chairman raises every member has generally a right to speak once but one only on each main motion and once on each amendment thereto but may move only one such amendment is before the meeting and all voting shall be by show or hands in the first place.

Motion and Amendments.

Strictly speaking a motion is proposition placed before a meeting which becomes only a resolution when adopted by the meeting; but the two terms are used almost synonymously.

Motions should always be couched in terms that are clear and definite and from ambiguity they should always be affirmative in form and commence with the word that so that when passed the record will read it was resolved that …. If the decision is to be immediately operative it should read be and is hereby done.

A motion must be within the scope of the notice convening the meeting and appropriate to the business of the meeting,

Generally a motion must be moved and seconded but although a chairman will usually require every motion to be seconded and will allow it to fall to the ground will not accept it for discussion if it does not find a seconder he is quite in order in putting an unseconded motion before the meeting unless the rules require otherwise. Motions are preferably committed to writing and handed to the chairman.

An amendment is a proposed alteration to a motion already under discussion by the meeting. It may take the form of adding words omitting words or substituting others or a combination of these it must conform to the general rules relating to motions except that it is not usually required to be seconded and it must not be a mere negation of the motion such as the insertion of word not. a chairman has a discretion in accepting amendments, but once accepted, discussion must centre on such amendment until it is voted upon, when, if passed, it is incorporated in the main motion discussion the reverts to the motion or any further amendment which is dealt with similarly when the whole matter has been sufficiently discussed the motion as finally amended is put to the meeting as the substantive motion and if passed is ultimately incorporated in the minutes. The mover of the motion is usually allowed a right to reply to the debate before the motion is put to the vote but the right must be claimed an amendment does not give the mover any such right.

The Formal Motions

These are motions designed to secure the termination, different, or prevention of discussion of the particular business before the meeting. Properly used, they fulfill their function of expediting the transaction of business; for which the meeting was called and hence are sometimes termed dilatory motions. As a consequence the chairman has a wide discretion as to whether he accepts such a motion.

The principal formal motions are:

a) ADJOURMENT OF THE MEETING. This may be moved by any member at the close of any speech. In the absence of any rule on the point it appears that a chairman must adjourn if the meeting resolves to do so; but the chairman may adjourn the meeting without asking a vote if he considers it necessary for the proper transaction of business, e.g, to await essential information. If he adjourns the meeting merely because things have taken a turn he does not like the meeting and no further notice need be sent out unless the regulations require, or unless the adjournment has been sine die (without fixing a day).

b) ADJOURMENT OF THE DEBATE. This amounts to no more than the deferment of one item until later in the proceedings ex. until a related item has been settled.

c) POSTPONEMENT. This amounts to the adjournment (of either a meeting or a motion) before discussion commences.

d) PREVIOUS QUESTION. This is moved either in the form I move the previous question or I move that the question be now not put the intention is to shelve discussion on the whole subject i.e. the main motion and this is achieved by deciding either to put the matter to the vote at once, or to drop the whole matter for the meeting. This decision is the previous question the P.Q can be moved only when the main motion is before the meeting, and discussion on it is permitted. If the question is passed, the meting drops the main motion and proceeds to the next business; if it is lost, the main motion is pit to the vote at once.

e) CLOSURE. This is usually in the form I move that the question be now put. It relates only to the particular motion or amendment before the meeting and is mostly used to curtail discussion or amendments. Hence, when moved and seconded, no discussion is allowed; the closure is put to the meeting and if, passed, the motion or amendment to "closured" is also put to the vote the mover if it is a main motion losing his right of reply. If the closure is lost discussion on the motion or amendment continues.

f) NEXT BUSINESS. A motion to "proceed with the next business" has the effect, if passed, of dropping the main motion before the meeting; and has no effect if lost.

Voting

The five usual methods of voting are:-

1. **Voice or Acclamation**. This can only be used where the meeting is practically unanimous.
2. **Show of Hands**. This is a method adopted at company meetings.
3. **Poll.** Literally a "counting of heads," but at company meetings each member has a number of votes laid down in the Articles, generally one vote for each share held.
4. **Ballot.** The members record their votes on voting papers, which they drip into a ballot box.
5. **Division.** The members pass out in separate rooms, being continued as they do so.

The chairman's declaration of the result of voting on a show of hands is conclusive unless a poll is demanded when the poll supersedes the original counting or unless there is some obvious error. At common law every member has a right to demand a poll; the demand must be made immediately upon the declaration of the result on the show of hands, and the chairman decides the time, manner and place of conducting the poll, subject to any regulations on the matter.

On a poll the votes of absent members may, if the regulations provide, be recorded by proxy.

Privilege

Statements which injure a person's reputation if made orally constitute slander; and if the statement causes damage or alleges the commission of a criminal offense the person slandered may recover damages.

It is, however, essential that speakers at meetings should be free to talk frankly, without fear of being called to account in

An action for slander; and accordingly, a person who in good faith makes a statement in pursuance of a duty to persons who have an interest in hearing the statement, or with a view to protecting his or his hearers interests is said to be protected by privilege. Such protection will be lost if the speaker is actuated by malice rather than duty or if he is a party to unnecessary publication e.g. he invites reporters to be present.

A "privileged occasion" is one where the above circumstances of duty and interest exist; meeting of directors and shareholders are consequently privileged occasions.

A written defamatory statement constitutes libel, and a civil action will lie without proof of damage. The protection of privilege applies as in the case of oral statements; consequently written reports made to a superior in the course of duty or placed before a board meeting are privileged if made in good faith, no matter how erroneous they may be.

To establish a prima facie case of libel it is necessary for the plaintiff to prove;

1. That the words complained of are defamatory and are therefore calculated to expose him to hatred, concept or ridicule or to cause him to be shunned or avoided;
2. That they refer to the plaintiff; and
3. That they are published by the defendant.

The following defenses are available in an action of defamation in speeches made at meetings or published reports thereof; unintentional defamation, fair comment (just and reasonable comment upon matters of the public interest, made without malice, privilege (absolute of qualified), and justification.

III

Kinds of Meetings

The following are the usual meetings held in connection with limited companies:-

The statutory meeting, being the first General Meeting of shareholders of a public company.

- Annual General Meeting.
- Extraordinary General meeting.

The above are meetings of the company and usually described as the statutory ordinary and extraordinary meetings respectively in addition there may be class meetings of the different classes of shareholder as well as

- Directors meetings, and
- Director's committee meetings.

Statutory meeting

The statutory meeting of a company is held in accordance with sect 130 of the companies act which enacts that every company limited by shares and every company limited by guarantee and having a share capital shall within a period of not less than one month or more than three months from the date at which the company is entitle to commence business hold a general meeting of the members of the company which shall be called a statutory meeting at least fourteen days before the day on which the meeting is to be held the directors have to forward a report must be certified by not less than two directors of the company the report must state

a) The total number of shares allotted distinguishing shares allotted as fully or partly paid up the extent to which they have been paid up, and in any case the considerations for which they have been allotted.

b) The total amount of cash received for all such shares, distinguished as aforesaid

c) An abstract of receipts and payment from shares and debentures and other sources up to date within seven days of the date of the report particulars of the balance in hand and an account or estimate of the preliminary expenses of the company.

d) Names addresses and descriptions of the directors auditors managers and secretary of the company

e) Particulars of any contract the modification of which is to be submitted for approval of the meeting, together with the particulars of the modification.

A private company need not forward or file a statutory report nor hold a statutory meeting.

The statutory meeting is frequently a mere formality but at such meeting shareholders have an opportunity of discussing any matters relating to the formation of the company or arising out of the report but unless notice has been given in accordance with the articles of association no resolution can be passed. At this meeting the directors produce a list showing the names descriptions and addresses of the members of the company and the number of shares held respectively. This list must be presented at the commencement of the meeting and be accessible to any member of the company during the continuance of it. Though seldom done in practice a statutory meeting may be adjourned from time to time and the adjourned meeting will have the same powers as the original meeting and any resolution of which notice has been given in accordance of the articles either before or subsequently to the former meeting may be passed. If the statutory report be not filed or the statutory meeting not be held the company may be wound up by the court but the latter may order the meeting to be held and the report be filed or make such other order as may be just.

Annual and Extraordinary General Meetings

By companies act, a general meeting of every company shall be held once at least in every calendar year, and not more than fifteen months after the holding of the last preceding annual general meeting. If the companies hold a general meeting within eighteen months of its incorporation or in the following year in default the company and every director secretary manager and other officer of the company who is knowingly a party to the default, is liable to a fine.

The act gives powers to shareholders to requisition of the calling of meetings and overrides any provisions made in the articles relating thereto. Shareholders representing not less than one tenth of such of the paid up capital as at the date of the deposit of the requisition carries the right of voting at general meetings may request the directors to convene what is termed an extraordinary general meeting the requisition has to state the objects of the meeting and be signed by the requisitionists and deposited at the registered office of the company. Such requisition may consist of several documents each duly signed by one or more of the requisitionists. If no meeting is called within twenty one days the requistionists, or any of them representing more than one half of the total voting rights of all of them may themselves convene the meeting but any such meeting shall not be held after three months from the date of deposit of the requisition. Any meetings called by virtue of the provisions of sect. 132 are to be called as nearly as possible in the same manner as meetings called by the directors any reasonable expenses incurred by the requisitionists owing to the director's default are to be paid by the company and charged against the defaulting directors.

Creditors Meetings

Though strictly meetings of a company, meetings of creditors of a company may be mentioned. They will be held when the company proposes to make a scheme of arrangement with its creditors under the act. Other meetings of creditors may take play in a winding up of companies.

IV

PROCEDURE BEFORE, AT, AND AFTER MEETINGS

BEFORE studying the contents of this chapter, one advised to read all matters referring to general meetings in any articles of association to which he may have access.

The Annual General Meeting is usually held some three or four months after the conclusion of the financial year; in fixing the date, regard must be had not only for the obligation to hold a general meeting not later than fifteen months from the preceding general meeting. Accounts shall be laid before the members not more than eighteen months after incorporation and subsequently once at least in every calendar year. The meeting must be held within nine months of the date to which the accounts are made up.

When the accounts have been completed and audited, the secretary will proceed to draft the director's report which should be a plain statement of the results of the trading for the year, followed by a statement as to the allocation of profits between dividends, reserves and "carry forward". The report usually ends with a note as to the retiring directors and so to the auditors – whether the directors seek re-election, and whether (as usual) the auditors are to continue to serve until the next annual general meeting.

The secretary will see that the hall which it is proposed to use for the meeting is available for the contemplated date, and will then be in a position to have set up in type the various documents required to be send to members' entitled to attend the meeting; these will consist of the notice convening the meeting, the director's report, the Balance Sheet and Loss Account, and the auditors' report on Profit and Loss Account and Balance Sheet and on the group accounts (if any). Proofs of these will be obtained and submitted to a duly convened Board meeting, which the auditors' representative will be invited to attend.

At this meeting the directors will approve the various documents, decide upon the dividend to be recommended, and they will discuss with the auditors' representative any amendment they desire in the form of accounts as they are to be printed. These matters settled, they will pass resolutions:

1. Authorizing the signing of the directors' report by the chairman or the secretary on their behalf;
2. authorizing the signing of the balance sheet by two directors on behalf of the Board
3. Convening the annual general meeting and authorizing the meeting in the Press; if necessary.
4. Giving instructions for the preparation dividend warrants, and the closing of the Registered of Member if that be the practice of the company.

As soon as this board meeting is concluded, the secretary will instruct the printers to proceed with all the necessary printing. It will generally be necessary to obtain two final proofs of the report and accounts and, after having them signed by the directors as arranged, to send them to the auditors, who will retain one copy for their fillies and return the other with the auditors' report thereon duly signed. This copy should be carefully preserved and should be available at the annual general meeting.

Envelopes will be prepared, ready to dispatch the report and accounts, etc., to all members of the company. Copies should be sent to the Nairobi stock exchange.

The secretary will put in hand the dividend arrangements and will prepare the chairman's detailed agenda for the meeting, and may be required to assist in the preparation of the chairman's speech.

Any member of a company entitled to attend and vote at a meeting may appoint another person to attend and vote in his place (who need not also be a member: needed, the member might send his advocated or his accountant, although in the case of meeting of a public company such a person has not the right to speak). The proxy forms should be checked and entered on a Proxy List as they are received; and the proxy forms and the list must be taken to the meeting.

Arrangements for the Meeting

On the day appointed for the meeting, the room must be prepared. Seats will be arranged for the chairman and the other directors at a tablet the head of the room and other seats will be provided for the general body of the shareholders. Where it is the practice to do so, copies of the agenda, reports and accounts of the directors and report of the auditors, will be placed on the seats for those attending. On the table, in front of the chairman, will be the fully detailed agenda, either on a loose leaf sheet or written in an Agenda Book, opened ready for the chairman's is. There will also be at hand the original signed copies of the report and accounts and auditors' report, correspondence to be read at the meeting, and the draft of the chairman's speech. The secretary will have at hand the Minute book, copy of the agenda (detailed), a copy of the report and auditors' report, the signed notice convening the meeting, and any other documents he may consider necessary. At every meeting he should have with a copy of the Memorandum and Articles of Association of the company.

There should also be Available is a good supply of writing materials. If the meeting is one important to the general public, reporters may be present, who should be afforded proper facilities.

The room should be open for the admission of shareholders at least half hour before the time appointed for commencing the meeting. As the shareholders enter the room, their attendance will automatically be recorded by their presenting admission cards. Where a card system is not adopted, arrangements should be made to take the signatures of those attending as they enter the room.

The chairman, and other directors, together with the secretary, and, where usual, other officers, e.g. the general manager, should be in their places before the advertised time of the meeting, so as to ensure its starting promptly. This applies also to any members of the staff who may be assisting.

If at the appointed hour the chairman finds that a quorum be not present, the meeting must stand adjourned, or as the Articles of Association direct. The Companies Act provides that, in the absence of provisions in the Articles, the quorum shall be: Three members personally present (in the case of a public company), or two members (private company).

The act provides for a quorum of "three members present in person," and provides, further, that if a quorum is not present within half an hour of the time fixed for the following week, and at the same place; and if at such adjourned meeting there is no quorum within half an hour of members present will constitute the quorum. If, however, it be a meeting specially convened upon the requisition of members, it must be dissolved.

Assuming that a quorum is present, the chairman will call upon the secretary to read the notice convening the meeting. There is no statutory requirement that this be done, but it is customary, as it calls the attention of those present to the business before them. The next item is the reading of the auditors' report upon the accounts; this duty is occasionally undertaken by the representative of the auditors but is more usually carried out by the secretary. The report and accounts of the directors come next, and it is usual for the chairman to ask the members, in view of the fact that these documents have been in their hands for the statutory period, to take them as read; a formal request to which there is seldom any dissent. He will proceed to move the adoption of the report and accounts by reading out the motion from the detailed agenda sheet. He then proceeds to deliver his "chairman's speech," in which he may review the year's trading, draw attention to any special points in the accounts, and possibly express an opinion of the prospects of the company for the immediate future. On the conclusion of his speech he calls upon the person named in the agenda to second the resolution. This gentleman (or possibly lady) will usually read the terms of the resolution from a slip which has been previously handed to him by the secretary, and may speak at length or otherwise on the matter. Following him, the shareholders, who are entitled to discuss the report and accounts, are asked by the chairman if they have any questions to ask or remarks to make in regard to have the report and accounts. This is the opportunity of dissatisfied and other shareholders, and where a satisfactory report has not been presented, numerous questions may be asked as to the affairs of the company, and an application may be made for an investigation into the company's affairs.

Putting the Resolution to the Meeting

A resolution is put to the meeting by the chairman saying, "Those in favor?" whereupon every member who vote for the resolution holds up a hand. If there is any case for believing a count to be necessary, the hands so held up will be counted by the chairman, with the assistance possibly of another director. The counting concluded, he will say, "Those against?" and the procedure will be repeated. Where it is a foregone conclusion that the resolution will be carried by a large majority, or the hands held up "in favor" show conclusively that the meeting is in favor of the resolution, the counting will be omitted unless, of course, it is necessary (as in a special resolution) to ascertain that the resolution has been passed by a certain majority. In such a case, however, there is usually a poll, as proxies have to be allowed for. The chairman may declare a resolution as carried, or by a certain majority, or where all have voted for the motion, carried unanimously; again, where no one has voted against the motion, carried men. Con. (nominee contradicente).

A member dissatisfied with the declaration may call for a count, or a recount, as the case may be; or he may resort at once to his right to demand a poll.

The companies Act, gives members the right to demand a poll at a general meeting on any question other than the election of the chairman or adjournment of the meeting.

Sect. 137(1) further states that a poll can be demanded by:-

"(I) Not less than five members having the right to vote at the"

"(ii) A member or members representing not less than one-tenth of"

"(iii) by a member or members holding shares in the company conferring a right to vote at the meeting, being shares on which aggregate sum has been paid up equal to not less than one-tenth of the total sum paid up on all the shares conferring that right."

Any provision in the Articles which might exclude such rights is void. Incidentally Table A, Clause 58 (b) provides that at least three members may demand a poll. This puts members who wish to dissent in an even stronger position for, as noted, the Act requires at least five members.

The demand is affected simply by a member rising and saying: "Mr. Chairman, I and... other members, making resolution just submitted to the meeting." A poll is in the nature of an appeal from the decision given to a show of hands, in which each member, irrespective of his holding, has number of votes set out in the Articles; Table A (clause 62), for example, provides that a member shall have one vote for every share he holds. Moreover, a poll will enable members present to record the votes of absent members whose authorizations they hold; and if the chairman decides that the poll be taken at a later date a larger proportion of the total membership may vote than if the poll is held immediately.

Proxies

The Companies Act states that an instrument appointing a proxy to vote at a meeting confers the authority to demand a poll. The word proxy is used to indicate both the person voting by proxy and the instrument authorizing him to vote; but the present writer prefers to use the terms as meaning only the person acting for another. A proxy may be any person, whether a member or not. A proxy appointed to attend and vote instead of a member of a private company has the same right as the member to speak at the meeting.

It is the duty of the secretary to observe his company's regulations with regard to proxies, particularly as to the proxy form, and delivery to the company. See clauses 67-73 of Table A. There is no stamp duty on proxy forms if for use at one meeting only or at any adjournment thereof, but a stamp of ten shillings is required if the form is for use at more than one meeting, as it then operates as a power of attorney. In this case the importance of stamping is apparent when it is realized that

1. An unstamped proxy form is invalid;
2. The validity of a resolution passed with its help may afterwards the disputed in the courts; and that
3. Any attempt made to use it involves a fifty pound penalty to the maker and user of it. "The instrument appointing a proxy" should be delivered to the company not less than forty-eight hours prior to the holding of the meeting at which the form will be used, or in the case of a poll; otherwise it is invalid. Other Articles may and often do provide for a shorter period. A proxy form not in order should be immediately returned.

The Act makes provision to afford members an opportunity of voting for or against a resolution.

When a poll is taken scrutinizers are often appointed by the meeting, whose business it is to report to the chairman the result of voting. Their work will be greatly facilitated by the secretary having at hand a list of proxies and the votes represented by them, and the Register of Members giving the holdings of those present at the meeting. The latter should be signed by the scrutinizers before being handed to the chairman.

Under the act no shareholder is allowed to vote at a general meeting if he be in arrears with calls, but a person of unsound mind, or in respect of whom an order has been made by any court having jurisdiction in lunacy, may vote, whether on a show of hands, or on poll, by his trustee, and such trustee may, on a poll; vote by proxy.

Records of the Meeting

During the progress of the meeting the secretary will have been taking brief notes of the proceedings. At a meeting of shareholders he will usually have little to do in this respect, beyond nothing that the business of the meeting has been disposed of properly. Against each item on the agenda he will put a tick to indicate that the matter referred to was passed. Where information has been asked for and promised by the chairman, he will make a note of this, also of any suggestions made by shareholders to the Board. Where the resolutions were passed in the form drafted by the secretary he will not need to copy them in his notes, nor will it be necessary for him to put the names of the proposers and secondary of resolutions therein, if they are those originally arranged for. If, of course, any instructions have been given at the meeting, it is the duty of the secretary to see that they are noted and carried out.

The secretary's first duty after meeting of shareholders, is to write up the record of the proceedings- the minutes- and as has been pointed out in a preceding chapter, everything material must be included in the minutes, before entry, should be submitted to the chairman for his approval, and after entry, the minutes should be laid before the next Board meeting and is signed by the chairman thereof. Where it is the custom, copies of the "Report of the Proceedings" will be printed and sent to the members. In the case of directors absent from the meeting and who have been re-elected, a notification should be sent to them. After such a meeting, too, there is the important work of posting the Dividend Warrants and of making up and forwarding the Annual Return.

Directors' Meetings

Although there is less formality at the meetings of the directors than at general meetings, it is nevertheless just as important that the requirements of the law of the company's Articles are strictly observed.

The Articles usually permit the directors to "regulate their meetings as they think fit." Unless, however, they have arranged to meet at fixed intervals and to dispense with notice, reasonable notice (say, two or three days at least) must be given of every meeting. If, however, all the directors are, in fact, present and agree, they can waive notice. This does not mean that because all the directors happen to be present, they can force one of their numbers, against his will, to take part in a meeting on the spot; but on the other hand, where they are all present and agree, they can hold a meeting in the most informal circumstances – e.g. on a railway platform, conversing through carriage window of a train about to depart. Table a (Clause 106) states that a written resolution, signed by all the directors for the time being entitled to receive notice of a directors' meeting, shall be valid and effectual without an actual meeting being held.

The Articles will state what the quorum for a Board meeting is, and it must be remembered that any business conducted without quorum, unless subsequently ratified, may be invalid. Moreover, there is a common law rule which prevents directors who are interested in a contract with the company both from voting on the matter in a Board Meeting and from being counted in the quorum." The Articles may however, amend this rule; but where a director abstains from voting on a contract because he is interested in it, it is as well to record the fact in the minutes, thus:

"Mr. A. B., being interested in the firm of C. And Co., abstained from voting."

Even if the Articles allow him to vote, an interested director must pen the companies Act; disclose at a Board Meeting the nature of his interest in any contract with the company. A general notice that he is a member of a particular firm or company, and is to be regarded as interested in any contract therewith, is sufficient.

The careful secretary will endeavor to keep in mind any interests so declared; for in the event of the absence of a dis-interested quorum, or the improper inclusion of such a director's vote, the contract may be avoided by the other party.

There will also be the preparation of the agenda and the forwarding of a copy of it, where the practice exists, to each director. With the notice, the secretary should send a note of reminder to any director whose duty it is to present any information to the meeting. In the preparation of the room a supply of writing materials should be placed before each director. The secretary will have at hand a copy of the Memorandum and the Articles of Association, the Minute Book, Directors' Attendance Book, copies of the agenda and all documents to be dealt with at the meeting. All papers can best be handled by the secretary if they are properly marked for identification. Each director should have a copy of the agenda. Most Articles of Association follow Table a (clause 86) in requiring directors present at a board meeting to sign the Attendance Book.

On the chairman taking his seat at the meeting begins usually by his explaining, where necessary, the absence of a director, after which the secretary is called upon to read the minutes of the last meeting. This done, the chairman says, "You have heard the minutes of the last meeting read. Will someone move that they be approved?"

The proposer and seconder of the resolution affirming the correctness of the minutes will, of course, be persons who attended the meeting to which the minutes refer. Where an error has been made it must be corrected.

After the minutes have been read, they are signed by the chairman, who, at the same time, should affix the date of the signing.

The next item on the agenda is usually "Matters arising out of the Minutes." This enables the chairman or other directors or, it may be, the secretary, to explain that certain instructions have been carried out, or to explain how far matters in a certain direction have progressed. The arrangement of the business should, as far as possible, be in accordance with the agenda, but the chairman may and often does alter this as he consider fit, particularly where by accident the secretary has not placed adjacent to each other matters having similar bearing. Another reason may be that the chairman wishes to ensure the consideration of some special matter. But it should be noted that, strictly speaking, the order of business should not be altered without the consent of the meeting.

The Secretary's Notes

The notes that the secretary will take of the proceedings of the directors' meeting will consist largely of decisions for incorporation in the minutes, and instructions which he will be responsible for carrying out. Naturally, the secretary will adopt the briefest of methods, when making his notes.

The initial after each note refers to the proposer and seconder.

At the conclusion of the meeting, the secretary will find that the list of instructions is frequently a large one, and if this be the case, he will be advised to have his "reminders" reproduced and written in triplicate form. One copy will be sent to the person concerned, at once, and another will be put in the secretary's "tickler" while the third copy will be retained for general reference. The "tickler" copy may be sent to the director as a further reminder of the duty he has to accomplish- with the notice convening the next meeting of directors. As soon as possible the minutes will be drafted for the chairman's approval and entered in the Minute Book.

In most Articles there will be regulations for the conduct of directors' meetings but apart from the meetings, members of committees may have a large amount of work to do before they can report to the general body of directors, who confirm or otherwise the recommendations they make in regard to the matter which they were specifically appointed to consider. It should be clearly understood however, that committees of the Board can be appointed only when the Articles authorize such appointment. The act provides for delegation of powers to committees.

V

NOTICES OF MEETINGS

An annual general meeting may be called by twenty-one days' notice in writing; and any other general meeting (except one for passing a resolution) may be called by fourteen days' notice. A meeting to pass a special resolution needs twenty one days' notice. Clauses 50-51 and 131-134 of Table A refer to notices for company meetings and provide for the above-mentioned notices exclusive of the day on which notice is served or deemed to be served, but inclusive of the day for which the notice is given and specifying the place, day and hour of meeting. Where special business is to take place, particulars must be stated in the notice, which must be sent to every shareholder or person entitled, but non-receipt of the notice by any member shall not invalidate the proceedings in any general meeting.

The Articles will usually provide that notices may be served personally or be sent by post to the registered address of the shareholder, and will be deemed to be properly served if the letter containing the notice is correctly addressed, prepaid and posted, unless proof of the contrary is established. Where the registered address of the shareholder is not in the country, he should supply an address within the country to which notices can be sent if this is possible (see clause 131 of Table A). Where shares are held jointly, the practice is to give notice to the one whose names appears first on the register. Secretaries will note that provision is made for the forwarding of the notices of meetings to persons entitles to shares in the consequence of death or bankruptcy of a member.

Notices of general meetings are invalid unless issued under the instructions of a properly constituted Board meeting, and the secretary should therefore see that the Board meeting at which it is decided to call a general meeting is itself validly convened, and that a quorum of directors is present.

Where share warrants to bearer have been issued, the company's Articles or regulations made there under usually provide for notices to the holders being given by advertisement or posting up the notice at the company's registered office.

The regulations with regard to the serving of notices for directors meetings are usually conspicuous by their absence, or comprehend in the words, "the directors may meet together for the dispatch of business, adjourn or otherwise regulate their meetings as they think fit." Nevertheless, the general rule is to forward written or unwritten notices a few days prior to the meeting taking place. In some companies no notice is served, the directors attending on a fixed day of a week or month. However, in practice, various papers for perusal by the directors are circulated before most Board meetings, which imply an imminent Board meeting even if formal notice is not enclosed. The business method is to have regulations so framed that written notice must be given at least two or three days before the meeting, with the reservation that a director or secretary may summon a meeting at any time, in a matter of urgency, at shorter notice.

Sect. 142 of the Companies Act. Cap 486 provides for a form of notice, called "special notice", to be given to a company in the case of certain resolutions which a member may wish to move. The proposed removal of a director over the age of 70 (Sect. 186) and the appointment of another auditor in place of retiring (Sect. 160), are requiring three cases of resolutions requiring special notice, which must not be less than twenty-eight days before the meeting. The directors must then include the resolution in the notice sent to share holders.

VI

AGENDA

Agenda means "things to be done". Its commercial interpretation is "business to be transacted at a meeting." It is simply a statement of matters that have to be discussed at a meeting. At every meeting the chairman and the secretary at least should have a copy of it; at directors meetings each director should have a copy; at meeting of shareholders, the usual provision is to include the agenda in the notice convening the meeting. It is of general advantage for particulars to be attached likewise to the notices convening the meetings of directors, so as to enable the latter to give some consideration to the matters referred to, before the meetings.

The more general practice in connection with director's meetings is to provide loose agenda sheets. Where an agenda book is used, the agenda items entered therein are placed before the chairman, and are regarded as the agenda. Those placed before the other directors or shareholders are copies only. As far as possible, matters of the similar character should be placed next to each other in any agenda, but in order in which the various matters will be dealt with at the meeting may be varied by the chairman, with the consent of those present.

There are two recognized method of preparing the agenda. Paper; one method is to enter the bare outline or summary of a various items to be considered on the left-hand side, leaving a wide margin on the right-hand side in which the chairman and secretary will record notes of the decision arrived by at the meeting, these notes forming the basis of preparation of the minutes. In the second method fuller details are given, including draft of the resolution to be submitted, and the agenda is so worded that, by the alteration of few words, the agenda paper will form the draft minutes, thus facilitating the subsequent writing up of the minutes book. This method is useful for routine work at Board meetings as the director can see at a glance exactly what business is to be transacted.

The agenda of the meeting of shareholders is where the company issues a printed report, attached to it, but for the purpose of the chairman and secretary, a more detailed form should be made.

Once the minutes have been written up and signed by the chairman as the correct, the agenda paper may be destroyed. This, in fact, is the recommended procedure, because retention to the agenda, with its rough notes, means that two separate records of the same meeting will exist, one being necessarily of a rather hurried and imprecise nature. Carefully prepared and accurate minutes are all that is required

VII
RESOLUTIONS

A resolution may be defined as a formal decision by vote of a legislative or other body; emotion is a proposal placed before a meeting with a view to its adoption as a resolution. Strictly speaking, therefore, motions and resolutions are not the same things. With regards to company meetings, however, motions whether agreed or not are usually referred to as resolutions, and the word is used throughout the company's act, and therefore in this book, in that sense.

In studying this section of the subject of the meetings the student must be very careful to note the kinds of resolutions, the reasons for them and the framing of them.

Resolutions in connection with meetings of shareholders are of three kinds, Viz. Ordinary or simple, extraordinary and special. Resolutions passed by meetings of directors are of one kind only, requiring merely to be passed by a simple majority or those voting; they are known as resolutions of the directors, or of the Board.

Ordinary Resolution

An ordinary resolution is one which is passed by a simple majority of those present who are entitled to vote and who vote at a meeting. Such a resolution is used for the disposal of any business not requiring, under the company's act or the article, to be passed by any other kind of resolution. It is thus used for all ordinary business at extraordinary general meetings.

Extraordinary Resolution

Extraordinary resolution is defined by the company's act. A resolution shall be an extraordinary resolution when it has been passed by a majority of not less than ¾ of such members as, being entitled so to do, vote in person or, where proxies are allowed, by proxy, at a general meeting at which notice specifying the intention to propose the resolution as an extraordinary resolution has been duly given.

Special Resolution

A special resolution shall be a special resolution when it has been passed by such a majority as it required for the passing of and extraordinary resolution and at a general meeting of which not less than 21 days notice, specifying the intention to propose the resolution as a special resolution, has been duly give; provided that, if it so agreed by a majority in number of the members having the right to attend and vote at such meeting, being a majority together holding not less than 95% in nominal value of the shares given that right, or, in the case of company not having a share capital, together representing not less than 95% of the total voting rights at that meeting of all the members, a resolution may be proposed and passed as a special resolution at a meeting of which less than 21 days notice has been given.

The procedure with regards to extraordinary and special resolution must be carefully followed in accordance with the Act. The matters to be specially borne in mind will be:-

1. Form the resolution
2. Proper notice to be served, which notice must contain the text of the resolution to be proposed.
3. If there are any proxy forms, to examine them, and to see that they are duly recorded.
4. That the chairman declares the result.
5. That the copy of such resolution be printed and forwarded to the registrar within 15 days from the passing thereof. This must be on the prescribed form.

The chairman's declaration that an extraordinary or a special resolution is carried is conclusive, without proof of the number or proportion of the votes for or against the entitled to vote may demand a poll.

Penalties attached in the following cases:-

1. Failure to forward to the registrar a printed copy of the resolution
2. Not attaching to the articles, or forwarding to a member when required, a printed copy of the special resolution.

Uses extraordinary or special resolution

An extraordinary resolution is mainly used in a voluntarily winding up where the company, by the reason of its liabilities, cannot continue its business, and it is advisable to wind up, and may be used to sanction certain other business connected with voluntary winding up, such as a delegation to creditors to point liquidators, or for sanctioning arrangements with creditors, etc.

Special resolution of frequent occurrence in a company practice. For example, they required, inter alia:-

a) To the change the name of the company.
b) To alter the articles.
c) To extend the "objects" clause of the memorandum.
d) In reduction of the capital.
e) In creating the reserve liability.

In addition, a company's article may stipulate that, in certain other cases, a special resolution required.

Framing of resolution

The majority of the resolution will be framed by the secretary, no matter to what meetings they refer; but they should be noted: unless the matter is perfectly cleared that is advisable for most special and extraordinary resolutions to be drafted by the company's advocate. When it is remembered for what purposes such as resolutions are purposed, it will be realized how possible it is to frame a resolution detrimental to the interest of the company. In many cases that matters to which such resolutions refer are such as will generally have to be dealt by an advocate, and in that event he will undoubtedly frame any necessarily resolutions.

Occasionally also, important decision of the Board in respect in which is essential that they are technically correct from the legal aspect, should be incorporated by the advocates in the resolutions to be passed by the Board; these may be resolutions with regard to reorganizations and other complicated changes of capital, etc. These observations apart, it will be found that capable secretary will have no difficulty in the framing of resolutions in general. In so doing, he must bear following facts in mind:-

1. The object of the resolution.
2. The necessity of framing it in language at once clear and unmistakable; any ambiguity might defeat the object of the resolution.
3. The resolution must be in accordance with the regulations of the company as defined by the memorandum and articles, and consonant with the requirements of the Company's Act, or any other Act affecting the matter. This means, inter alia, that the effect of it must not be ultra virus i.e. something beyond the power of the company to adopt.
4. The particular wishes of the chairman or the directors of the company.

In regard to this last, it is a practice in some companies to submit to the chairman all resolutions to be purposed before the meeting, where possible.

Bearing the above matters in mind, the secretary will proceed in the framing of the resolution thus:-

1. Marshal the facts, in having done so-
2. Summarize them, and-
3. Incorporate them in a plainly worded and decisive statement.

Rescission

A resolution is rescinded at a meeting at which it has been passed. If a cancellation is decided upon, the resolution should be rescinded at a later meeting.

Majority

The word "majority" has two meanings:

a) A number which is more than half of the whole number.
b) The number by which the votes of one side exceed those of the others.

The meaning of the word "majority" according to the Company's Act is the greater number.

VIII
MINUTES

A MINUTE as defined in the dictionary is "A note assist the memory." In business matters, minutes are records of proceedings at meetings. Limited companies are required to "Cause minutes of all proceedings, all proceedings at meetings of its directors, and, where there are managers to be entered in the books kept for that purpose;" and further, "Any such minute purporting to be signed by the chairman of the meeting at which the proceedings were had, or, by the chairman of the next succeeding meeting, shall be evidence of the proceedings." Where such minutes are not kept, the company and every officer in default shall be liable to the default fine. Apart from the necessity of observing the above requirements it will be evident to all that records of proceeding must be kept in order to "assist the memory" of the directors and shareholders of the company and in regards to the matter they regularly discussing.

Kinds of Minutes

An examination of the minutes that is of the records proceedings of limited companies will reveal the fact that such minutes contain-

1. Statement of fact or circumstance, sometimes called Minutes of Narration and
2. Resolutions or statements of decision.

A Minute of Narration may either stand alone or be attached to a resolution as the circumstances determine.

The Minute Book

Separate books should be used for minutes of shareholders of directors and the committee meetings, each with sheets consecutively numbered, and provided with an extension index. The later will refer to all the minutes recorded, but in place of this the card index system may be and often is used. Minutes relating to more than one meeting should not be entered on the same page. Many forms contain only two divisions, one for the number of minutes and the other, the larger portion, for all other particulars. Sometimes, the names of proposer and seconder are given. In a column marked "subject", a very brief statement of what the minutes refers to will be given, while in the "Reference Index" column will be entered a reference to the pages of the book which, before and after the minute referred to contain any reference to the same subject matter. This index will be used only in matters of importance occurring frequently. Instead of referring to pages, the number might refer to minutes, but it would be desirable in that case to have the matter numbered consecutively throughout the book.

Minute Books of general meetings must be kept at the registered office of the company, and for at least two hours each day is open to the inspection free.

Members are entitled to be furnished with copies.

Before minutes are recorded in the Minute Book, it is a good plan, where possible, to show a rough draft to the chairman, for his approval. This will usually do away with the necessity of having to alter the minutes where the secretary has misunderstood some direction of the minutes. Where the mistake has been made in entering the minutes, before they are signed it will be better for secretary to rule neatly through the error, and re-enter the particulars correctly. He should get his chairman to initial the deletions when the minutes are being signed. If the minutes are being typed on unnumbered loose-leaf sheets, it is, of course, possible to re-type them. No erasures of any kind must be made. After the minutes are signed, the proper course, where a mistake has been made, is to pass a resolution rescinding the minute referred to, making the corrected on accordingly.

Whilst a narration should precede a resolution wherever necessary to explain the circumstances in which it came to be passed, the secretary should avoid so far as possible the minting of reason; for the reason which actuated one director to vote for a resolution maybe the very reason why another director voted against it. Moreover, it is usual to record only the fact that the resolution was passed, without indicating the numbers voting for or against; but it is generally accepted that a director who disagrees with any particular decision has the right, if he wishes, to have the fact of his voting against, or abstention from voting, recorded in the minutes.

Proposals which were not accepted are usually omitted from minutes, unless the matter happens to be of exceptional importance.

Reading the Minutes

The customary practice is for the minutes of one board meeting to be read at the next board meeting and, after being read, the chairman asks his co-directors if the minutes as read are correct record. Upon their assent being obtained, the chairman adds his signature and the date. The minutes of annual general meetings are usually approved at the next succeeding board meeting. Where this course is adopted no reference is made at the annual general meeting to the previous year's minutes.

IX

REPORTS

THE company secretary will have to frame the following among other reports-

The Statutory Report.

The report of the directors to the shareholders on results of trading-commonly known as the Annual Report.

Report or summary of the proceedings of important meetings of the company, where such are provided for the issue to the shareholders or to the press, e.g. report of the annual general meeting.

Reports of committees of directors on special matters.

Method of Framing Reports

After some study of various reports, it will be found that the information therein given can generally be placed under certain "heads." As an example, take the report of the directors-the Annual Report to the Shareholders. The following headings would cover important issues.

1. General reference to accompanying accounts.
2. Prospects of the company.
3. Extension of the company's business or business premises, new departures, amalgamation with or absorption of other companies.

4. Reference to increase of capital, etc.
5. Directorate and staff changes.
6. Reference to the auditors and their work and remuneration.
7. Proposals with regard to dividends, reserves, etc/
8. The accounts attached\

These "heads" are, of course, of a general character, but from them they may be built up any annual report, mentioning the matters as apply, and others of a nature peculiar to the company. The report accompanies the audited statement of accounts which every company is required to send, not less than 21 days before the annual general meeting, to every member and debenture holder entitled to receive notices of general meetings. A common practice is to print the report in the "fold" of the accountants, and to endorse the notice on the outside fold. On the front of the report there is usually a statement giving names of the directors, bankers, advocates, auditors, and secretary of the company, etc.

Reports or Directors' Committees

Committees of directors may be classed thus-

Standing or permanent committees.

Committees which exist only for the purpose of undertaking special business.

Not all companies have standing committees, and some companies have no committee at all. The articles must authorize the formation of a committee before it can be appointed.

The most familiar instance of a standing committee of a limited company is a Finance Committee. There are also Transfer or Registration committees that deal with all the matters referring to the transfer and registration of shares, etc.

Reports of Committees of Directors on Special Matters

There are of very varied character, but the following brief list will give an idea of the matters often reported on-

The desirability of opening business in another marketing area.

The advisability of erecting new premises.

The purchase of another business undertaking.

To consider the raising of additional capital.

To inquire into the management of certain departments.

To co-operate with other business undertakings in the promotions of legislation in a certain direction.

The establishment of a Pensions Funds for employees.

In arranging a set of "heads" as guidance when formulating the report, consideration must be given to the particular nature of the matter to be reported on. Thus, in some cases the following "heads" would be suitable-

1. The terms of the resolution, that is, a copy of the resolution of the directors, with the date when passed.
2. A statement of the inquires made or particulars of advice sought for and from whom.
3. Tests and results of any tests, where made (as in witnessing the tests of strengths of materials, yarns, cloths, etc,' or Again, materials used in the construction of erection of buildings, etc.)
4. The general finding of the committee, and where the members are divided in their opinion, the nature and causes of the division of opinion.

X

DIRECTORS

DIRECTORS are the members of a company who are appointed by the general body of shareholders to manage its affairs. Normally, they will be persons who are not capable of performing the duties delegated to them but at the same time have the full confidence of the shareholders. Standing as it were in the shoes of the latter, they attempt to represent their views in so far at least as successful management and trading is concerned. They are in sense active partners in the business; consequently they have a large amount of freedom of action. Notwithstanding the latter statement, however, directors are bound by the regulations of the company, and they are the persons responsible for carrying out of all matters required by such regulations. Their duties, therefore, are simply to carry out the objects for which the company was established which in most cases are to trade and make profits, and thus produce a dividend for the shareholders. In their capacity as directors they can act only as a Board, and consequently all their decisions should preferably be taken at board meetings, properly constituted and conducted according to the law relating to such meetings and the articles of the company; but where the Articles allow, the board may delegate duties to committees consisting of one or more directors.

Appointment of Directors

Every public company must have at least two directors, and all private companies must have at least one director. (A sole director must also be the secretary). So far as the secretary is concerned he must see with regard to every director or proposed director-

1. That he is capable of acting;

2. That he holds or will hold the necessary qualification in regard to shares, where such a condition is imposed in the Articles;

3. That his appointment as a director is properly made in accordance with the company's Articles.

In the case of public companies, every director is to be appointed by separate resolution agreeing to a "combined" appointment is passed unanimously.

In the case of the public company, every director appointed by the Articles, and every director and proposed director named in a prospectus issued within an year of the company becoming entitled to commence business, must also have signed the Memorandum of Association for the necessary qualification shares (if any), or taken such shares from the company and paid or agreed to pay for any such qualification shares, or made, and delivered to the Registrar a statutory declaration to the effect that he is already qualified. There is no legislation making it compulsory for a director to hold shares in the company, but most articles stipulate a share qualification.

Whilst the first directors who are named in the Article or prospectus must be qualified before being named, a director who is subsequently appointed must obtain his qualification shares within two months after appointment, or a less period if the Article requires it. If he fails to obtain, or to retain, his qualification shares, he automatically vacates office; and if he continues to act as a director he is reliable to a fine.

When the first directors are not appointed by the Articles they are usually appointed by the subscribers to the memorandum either at a resolution at a meeting, or by a document which they have all signed.

Subsequently, any vacancies occurring in the directorate are filled in accordance with the Articles, usually at the annual general meeting of the shareholders. Directors of private companies are often "life" directors, but in public companies the common rule is for one-third of the directors to retire at each annual general-meeting, those retiring being eligible for re-election by the meeting, and usually seeking it. Vacancies occurring at other times, e.g. by resignation or death, are known as casual vacancies and under most Articles such vacancies can be filled immediately by the remaining directors. Such appointments need the confirmation of the members at the next annual general meeting.

Remuneration of Directors

Directors are usually remunerated by fees fixed by the Articles or voted by resolution of a general meeting. These fees must be subject to income tax, and details must be disclosed in the annual accounts, which must also show fees in respect of a directorship of a subsidiary. The accounts must disclose separately the amount of the directors' other emoluments, namely, salary, expense allowance, any contribution paid in respect of each director under any pension scheme, and the estimated money value for any other benefits received by him otherwise than in cash. The accounts must also show the aggregate of directors' or past directors' pensions, and of any compensation to directors or past directors in respect of loss of office.

Where Articles mention a definite sum per annum as remuneration, directors serving only part of a year are not entitled to a proportionate fee. The wording is, therefore, generally such as to indicate an accruing remuneration from day to day.

Resignation and Removal of Directors

Under the Companies Act, a director of a public company must retire at age 70 unless approval is given in general meeting for him to continue beyond that age, and special notice is given of the resolution to be passed.

A director may also lose office through retirement by rotation, death, resignation, or by operation of the Companies, if

i)   He fails to obtain (within two months of his appointment), or to retain, his qualification shares (Sect.183);

ii)   He becomes bankrupt and the court does not grant him leave to act (Sec.88); or

iii) He has been guilty of fraudulent trading or any fraud in five years.

In addition, the Articles of a company often stipulate that other events shall disqualify a director. Clause 88 of a table that provides that: A director shall vacate office on the following additional grounds:-

If he becomes bankrupt or makes an arrangement or composition with his creditors generally; or is found of unsound mind; or has been absent for more than six months from the Board Meetings without the permission of the other directors.

The Act, gives power to remove a director by an ordinary resolution of which special notice has been given.

Assignment of Office

The Companies Act, provides that any assignment of his office by a director that may be permitted by the Articles or by any agreement entered into between any person and the company for empowering a director to assign his office is not effective unless and until it is approved by a special resolution of the company. On effective assignment the assignee becomes a full director in his own right. Were it not for the provision, and this might not always be in the best interests of the company and its shareholders.

Alternate Directors

A temporary delegation of the duties of a director may be made, if the Articles of Association permit, effective on notification to the company, no statutory sanction being necessary. The appointment is usually made by a director who, because of illness, absence abroad, or other reason, is unable to continue his duties. Such appointment is usually subject to the approval of the majority of the other directors.

An alternate director is not entitled to fees from the company-he will usually be paid by the director whose place he is taking-and he acts only in the absence of his appointer, who can revoke the appointment at any time. Furthermore it automatically lapses if the appointer ceases to hold his office. Alternates do not usually need any share qualification. Notice of appointment must be filled with the Registrar.

Register of Directors and Secretaries

A "Register of Directors and Secretaries" must be kept, containing the names, addresses, occupations and other particulars of such persons, a copy of which must be sent to the Registrar (with the Annual Return), to whom also must be notified from time to time (within fourteen days) any changes among the directors or secretaries. This is effected by filling a Return by the appointment by the director of the alternate, and such appointment becomes effective on notification to Directors and to Secretaries, which is a copy of the Register of Directors and Secretaries so far as existing officers are concerned. The register must be open for inspection daily by the members of the company without charge, and by any other person on payment regarding the taking of copies.

Register of Directors' Shareholdings

A Register of Directors' Shareholdings, etc., must be kept with the object of giving publicity to the dealings by directors in the shares and debentures of the companies on whose boards they serve: this is required to comply with the Companies Act. The Register must show regarding each director the number, description and amount of shares or debentures of the company, of its subsidiaries, of its holding company and of its fellow subsidiaries. It is kept at the company's registered office, and must be open to inspection of members and debenture holders for at least two hours a day for a period beginning fourteen days before the annual general meeting and ending three days thereafter.

Throughout this period the register must be open for inspection during business hours, subject to such reasonable restrictions as the company may, by its Articles or in general meeting, impose so that not less than two hours each day be allowed for inspection. The Register must be produced at the annual general meeting and be available for inspection throughout the meeting by any person attending.

Loans to Directors

The Companies Act provides that it shall not be lawful for the company to make a loan to pay any person, who is its director or director of its holding company, or to enter into any guarantee or provide any security in connection with a loan made to such by any other person.

XI

APPLICATION AND ALLOTMENT

WHEN the prospectus has been printed, and a copy (signed by every person named therein as a director or proposed director, or by his agent authorized in writing) has been deposited with the Registrar of Companies, supplies may be issued to the company's bankers, who will distribute it to all their branches, and to the brokers and any other persons who have underwritten any part of the issue. These people will Endeavour to interest their clients in the issue, and may be mentioned that it is customary to pay brokerage to brokers, bankers and other agents on all shares allotted through their introduction.

Prospectuses so distributed will be accompanied by a form of application, and it should be noted that the Companies Act, the deposit which accompanies an application must not be less than 5 per cent of the nominal amount of shares applied for. Where shares of different classes are being offered simultaneously, it is usual to issue separate application forms for each class, of different colors, so that they can be readily sorted when, at a later stage, they are received in the company's office.

Arrangements will also be made for the prospectus to be printed in the financial and more important daily newspapers; it may be necessary to print a form of application in the advertisement. These applications will necessarily be small and difficult to handle, and it is therefore a good plan to have ready, in advance, sheets of paper of the same size as the ordinary application forms, on which the applications cut from newspapers may be pasted as soon as they are received by the company.

The prospectuses and application forms themselves will contain clear directions as to the date on which the lists will be opened for subscription and as to whether applications are to be sent to the company's bankers, or brokers, or to an issuing house which has undertaken the office work, or to the registered office of the company itself. The most common method is to arrange with the company's bankers to receive the applications and to the registered office of the company itself. The most common method is to arrange with the company's bankers to revive the applications and to detach and clear the cheques which accompany them, the rest of the work being carried out in the company's own office; and in the following description it will be assumed that this arrangement has been effected.

It must be borne in mind that an issue of shares involves a very large amount of work, which- especially if the issue is a popular one and quickly over-subscribed- must be carried out with the maximum speed. Yet no work demands greater accuracy; and consequently the available office staff must be well organized beforehand, divided into sections each under an experienced senior, and each section thoroughly instructed in its duties. It may be necessary to engage additional help; there are men who regularly accept temporary work of this nature and whose experience makes them invaluable assistants. Shares or debentures are to be dealt in on the stock exchange; application for permission must be made before the third day after the first issue of the prospectus in accordance with the Companies Act.

Closing the Lists

On the morning that the lists are opened, constant touch must be maintained with the bank, who will list the applications as they detach the remittances there from and will have the lists and application forms ready for collection at short intervals by a clerk from the company. No proceedings can be taken on applications made in pursuance of a prospectus until the beginning of the third day after that on which the prospectus is first issued or such later time (if any) as may "the times if the opening of the subscription lists."

Where the issue is not immediately oversubscribed, the directors, through the secretary, will maintain communication with the bank, which will be able to report from time to time with the total money received, from which the number of shares applied for can be quickly calculated. An application for shares or debentures of a company which is made in pursuance of a prospectus is not revocable until after the expiration of the third day after the time of opening the subscription lists. After that time an application may be withdrawn if the applicant's withdrawal is received before the allotment letter is posted. (An application is an offer to take shares, and an allotment is the acceptance of that offer, the allotment letter being the usual method of notification.)

Dealing with the Applications

Each batch of applications collected from the bank is checked with the bank's list which accompanies it; and the applications are then entered on application sheets. There are three ways in which the entering may be carried out:

1. To number the applications in the haphazard order in which they are received from the bank and then to enter them on the sheets in that order; or
2. To rearrange them in alphabetical order of the names of the applicants and to commence a new application sheet for each letter; or
3. To sort them into groups according to the number of shares applied for

The last mentioned is now recognized as generally the most convenient; it will be found that most applicants have applied for round numbers of shares, e.g. 25, 30, 50 or 100, and if all applications for the same round number are entered in the columns will be identical, and the totaling of the number of shares applied for thereon and the calculation of the money amounts to be inserted will be greatly facilitated. Moreover, it is frequently desired to make, say a full allotment to applicants for not more than 100 shares, and to make only a proportionate allotment to others; and the information necessary to consider the matter is available only if the sheets have been compiled in this manner. Whichever sequence is adopted, the sheets will be distributed amongst the staff, each section being charged with entering up and totaling a definite group of applications, e.g. numbers

1-100 shares. As the sheets are filled they should be totaled and checked; and the totals numbers of shares applied for and total money paid should be carried to a summary sheet.

Allotting the Shares

As soon as the summary is completed and checked, it is placed before the directors, who decide the basis of allotment. If the issue is oversubscribed, it is clear that some or all of the applicants will have to receive only a proportion of the number of shares they have applied for; or that some may receive no allotment at all. If under-subscribed, the applicants of the underwriters will have to be inserted on the lists to make up the deficiency. The directors having made their decision, the number of shares to be allotted to each applicant is inserted against his name on the application sheet. When these sheets are totaled, the number of shares allotted on each sheet is also carried to the summary and there totaled. As soon as the summary is checked, it is placed before the directors.

On this occasion it is essential that the directors meet as a Board or as an Allotment Committee, if the Board has so delegated the duty of allotment. The chairman will sign the summary, and each allotment sheet should be signed or initialed by a director as to how the shares will be allotted.

This resolution will be duly entered by the secretary in the Board or Committee Minute Book.

Allotment cannot be made if within forty days after the first issue of the prospectus the conditions regarding minimum subscription and the receipt of the application moneys have not been fulfilled, otherwise all moneys received must be returned within forty-eight days of the first issue of the prospectus. The directors will be jointly and severally liable to repay the money with interest after the forty-eighth day has expired, If however, a director can prove that the loss of the money – if any – was not due to any misconduct or negligence on his part, he will not be liable.

It must be stressed that what has been stated above applies only to an issue on the formation of a company. It will be obvious that a company may well have several new issues during its lifetime, and in these cases there is no "minimum subscription," failure to reach which will involve the return of the application money. Nor does a "minimum subscription" apply to a statement in lieu of prospectus. This document is commonly known filed by a successful private company which seeks to extend its capital and its membership by becoming a public company. In such cases the members of the former private company and their friends will be only too pleased to subscribe to the increased capital of a company that has operated successfully, perhaps over a period of years. Hence no appeal to the public is deceived.

Letter of Allotment and of Regret

Immediately after the directors have passed the resolution of allotment, the secretary should lose no time in forwarding letters of allotment to those whom shares have been allotted, and letters of regret where no allotment has been made.

The bank should have a copy of the letters of allotment and of regret, together with a complete list of the cheques to be paid in respect of moneys returned, these cheques being printed at the foot of the letters of regret.

The same division of labor as arranged in connection with the making up of the application and allotment lists will be necessary in regard to the dispatch of the letters of allotment and regret. Where the applications have been entered according to the number of shares applied for and no allotment is made, for example, to applicants for not more than 50 shares, the sheets for such applicants can be passed immediately to one section of the staff for the preparation of letters of regret; whilst the remaining sections can proceed to fill in allotment letters from the remaining sheets. All letters whether of allotment or of regret should be careful checked before being dispatched, as in other matters worth checking is necessary, should not be done by the person or persons who did the original work; that is to say, all checking should be independent. The most expeditious plan is for one person to read out the particulars in the above letters, whilst a second person is making comparison with the allotment lists. The completed letters are inserted in the envelopes. The use of window envelopes will obviate both the necessity of checking and the possibility of wrong insertion. Care should be taken in posting the letter of allotment, for and completion of this the contract becomes binding both on the company and on the allottee; and responsible person should be required to check the sealed envelopes against the allotment sheets, to attend the postings and to certify the time, place and date of posting on the allotment sheets itself.

After the posting of the allotment letters, matters demanding early attention include the making out of checks for brokerage and underwritings commissions, and arrangements for providing split allotment letters on request.

Renunciation and Splitting

It is now usual to provide facilities for renunciation with letters of allotment. The object is to facilitate dealings in the new shares without the trouble or expense of getting transfer registered.

If a shareholder wishes to divide his rights amongst two or more persons, he returns the letter of allotment to be cancelled, receiving in exchange two or more letters as required. These are termed "split" letters.

The receipt of renounced letters and the issue of splits are usually recorded on the allotment sheet for information when writing up the registrar of members there from.

Return of Allotment

The Companies Act requires that when a company limited by shares, or a company limited by guarantee and having a share capital, makes any allotment of its shares, the company must within one month thereafter file with the registrar of companies a "Return of Allotments. The same section should be noted with respect to the filing of all contracts for shares agreed as fully or partly paid, otherwise than for cash. The secretary should see that such contracts are filed with the Registrar before any allotment of shares is made. There is a heavy penalty for making default knowingly, but the Court has power to grant relief and extend the time for filing if the omission was accidental or inadvertent. The allotment is not invalid simply by failure to make the necessary return.

When finally dealt with, the allotment sheets are usually bound.

Irregular Allotment

The Act forbids the allotment (in the case of a first issue to the public) of any shares until applications to the amount of the minimum subscription have been received and (in the case of any issue) unless application moneys amounting to at least 5 per cent of the nominal amount of shares have been received. The Act forbids any allotment unless a prospectus or statement in lieu has been filed. Any allotment made contrary to the provisions of these sections is voidable at the instance of the applicant within one month after the statutory meeting, or where the allotment is made after the statutory meeting, within one month after the allotment, whether the company has then gone in to liquidation or not.

A company and its officers are liable to heavy fines if an allotment is made in connection with a prospectus issued to persons other than existing members or debenture holder before the beginning of the third day after that on which the prospectus is first issued or such later time stated in the prospectus.

The Companies Act, states that any allotment is void where a prospectus states that application has been or will be made for permission for the shares to be dealt in on the Stock Exchange, but where in fact the permission has not been applied for before the third day after the issue of the prospectus.

XII

THE REGISTER OF MEMBERS

THE Companies Act requires that every company shall keep, in one or more books, a register of its members. This can be kept at the registered office or at the office where the register made up. Notice must be sent to the registrar of the place where it is kept, and of any change in that place, unless it is and always kept at the registered office. The following particulars must be entered in the register-

1. Names and addresses of members, and in case of a company having a share capital, a statement of the shares held by each member, distinguishing each share by its number, so long as the share has a number and of the amount paid or agreed to be considered as paid on the shares of each member.
2. The date which each person has entered in the register as a member.
3. The date at which any person ceased to be a member.

Every company having more than fifty members must, unless the Register of Members is in such a form as to constitute in itself an index, keep an index of the names of the members of the company sufficient to enable each member's account to be found. This index must be at all times kept at the same place as the register of members. Any alteration made in the Register of member must also be recorded in the records within fourteen days.

A person signing the Memorandum of Association is deemed a member on the incorporation of the company. Other persons who have agreed to be members become members as soon as their names are placed on the register. The companies act, does not specify any particular for of register, so long as it comprises one or more "books" (and this term has been held legally to include loose leaf systems), so that the secretary may adopt any form suitable for his particular company, so long as he includes therein the particulars above noted. Small companies sometimes make use of bound registers (special books can be obtained from law stationers in the form one volume pages specially ruled for the register of members, register of directors and secretaries, copies of annual return, etc.), but practically all companies with more than a few members keep their Register of Members in loose leaf form in a series of binders. This enables closed accounts to be removed to a separate file. A separate index will not be necessary if a single sheet is confined to one shareholders account and the accounts are strictly arranged in alphabetical order. Some Safe guards are necessary, when a loose leaf register is kept, to prevent fraud by the indentation of re-written leafs in the place of correct ones. The binders must be fitted with locks, and blank loose leaves should be numbered and kept under lock and key by a responsible official, who should keep record of all sheets issues, and to whom any spoilt sheets should be returned.

There are several ways of providing for shares of different classes. Probably the most satisfactory one is to use different colored sheets for each class, so that where a shareholder has shares of three different kinds his three sheets will be inserted in the binder together. In that case only the first sheet need contain the detailed heading and notes, and considerable labor is saved in dealing with changes of address, etc., whilst the convenience of having all the records of a shareholder adjacent to one another is obvious but there may, nevertheless, be circumstances in which it is more convenient to have separate registers for the different classes. A further method is to have additional columns; or, again, the ruling for ordinary shares may be printed in the upper half, and the ruling for preference shares in the lower half.

It is essential to have the Register of Members complete as soon as possible after allotment. When rights of renunciation have been given, it will obviously be impartibly to bring the Register into use until the last date for receiving renunciations has passed; although the writing up of sheets may be put in hand previously.

Registration of Birth Certificates, probate, etc.

A duty in which must receive careful attention is the entering, at the head of a shareholder's account, of any notes affecting the account. Documentary authority for any such note must be received and recorded. These notes may concern the exhibition of death certificates, of probate and letters of administration, naming the executors and administrators; of marriage of a female shareholder, etc.

Rectification of Register

By Companies Act, a person whose name has been removed from the register without sufficient cause may apply to the court to have his name replaced on such a register. Where "default is made or unnecessary delay takes place in entering on the register the fact of any person having ceased to be a member," application may be made to the court to rectify the register.

Examination of the Register

The company Act, states that the register of members shall be open to inspection of any member gratis, and of any person on the payment of a fees for each inspection as the company in general meeting may prescribe. Inspection must take place in business hours, and whilst "reasonable restrictions" may be imposed on such inspection, two hours per day may be allowed for it, except for it where the books are closed in accordance with the provisions of the Act/ A copy of the register or any part thereof may be obtained by any person on payment of such sum as the company may prescribe, for every hundred words or fractional part of a hundred words required to be copied. Refusal to grant the inspection, or to give the copy as above, makes the company reliable in respect to each offence to a fine. The directors and the managers are likewise personally reliable. An immediate inspection of the register may be made by the court.

Closing the Register

The companies Act, cap gives power to close the register for a period or periods not exceeding thirty days in each year. Companies may take advantage of this provision when the dividend warrants are being prepared immediately prior to the Annual General Meeting. The closing of the register also enables lists of shareholders entitled to dividends to be prepared, allows proxy papers to be present at the meeting. Many companies, however, find it unnecessary to close their Registers of Members.

Dominion Register

A "Dominion" register may be kept by a company having a share capital, whose objects comprise the transaction of business in a colony or other part of the dominions, and which is authorized by its Articles to keep such a register. Notice must be given to the Registrar of any office where such a register kept, also of a change of office, and of its discontinuance.

A duplicate of every dominion register must be kept at the office where the principal register is kept, and must be kept posted up from copies of the entries transmitted for the purpose. This duplicate forms part of the principal register, and is subject to all the statutory requirements as to inspection and copies.

Should it be necessary for share entries to be transferred to a dominion register, it is usual for the shareholder to apply for such a transfer, surrendering his share certificate and paying the prescribed fee. The procedure then includes the cancellation of the certificate and the issue of a receipt therefore, the advising of the branch office of the transfer so that the shareholder's account in the principal register.

Termination of Membership

Membership of company may cease by:

a) Sale and/or transfer of shares,
b) Forfeiture of the shares, if authorized by the articles,
c) Valid surrender of shares,
d) Death, Bankruptcy, or becoming of unsound mind, if the shares are disclaimed or transferred by the personal representative,
e) Rescission of the contract to make shares, because of fraud, misrepresentation, or mistake,
f) Repudiation of partly-paid shares by an infancy,
g) The winding up of the company,
h) Redemption of redeemable preference shares when such are the sole holding,
i) Exchanging share certificate for share warrant; and by other means.

XIII

SHARE CERTIFICATE

The Companies Act, states that "a certificate under the common seal of the company, specifying any shares held by any member, shall be prime facie evidence of the title of the member of the shares." Sect. 82 of the Companies Act requires certificates to be completed and ready for delivery within two months after allotment or lodgment of the transfer of any share, etc., unless the conditions of issue of share provides otherwise. The Articles usually provide for a first certificate to be given free of charge to every member whose name is entered on the register. It is issued in exchange for allotment letters and bankers' receipts for the amounts paid. In the first place, a single certificate is issued to include all shares of one class held by any one member. To joint holders, only one certificate is issued.

If the settlement and quotations be sought on the stock exchange, the form of certificate will have to be approved by the committee of the exchange. Forms will vary, too, in the matter of shares being paid up or only partly paid up. The printed forms of certificate are usually delivered to the secretary in book form, and in three parts, each part being detachable by perforated line. These parts are the counterfoil, the certificate proper, and the receipt or form of acknowledgement of the receipt of the certificate of the member. Each part will be numbered with the same number, and the pages of the certificate book will be consecutively numbered. If the certificates are not in book form, they can be more expeditiously dealt with, several persons entering the necessary particulars thereon simultaneously, from the allotment list. Certificates in respect of different styles or colors.

The facsimile share certificate is one that would be issued in respect of shares not fully paid. On the back of it there would be a printed form or forms on which to indicate the payment of calls.

Where the full nominal amount of shares is payable during a period of a few months from the date of allotment, it is a convenient practice to defer the issue of certificates until the shares are fully paid, but the prospectus must so provide. This practice avoids the large amount of clerical work involved in issuing certificated for partly paid shares and, later, endorsing thereon the payment of various calls.

Issue of the Certificates

The certificates are written up from the allotment sheets as soon as the period renunciation has expired or from the Register of Members if it has been completed. In either case, the distinctive numbers of shares comprised in each certificate are first worked out and inserted on the Allotment sheets or Register, and the last number checked with the total number of shares to be issued. When completed by the secretary's staff they should be checked; frequently this is done by the company's auditors, who give a report that the certificates are in order for sealing and issue. It is an additional check on the whole of the work if the certificates written up from the allotment sheets are checked to the Register of Members, or if prepared from the Register of Members, they are checked to the allotment sheets. This is a double check that should be employed whenever possible. The certificates and auditor's report are then submitted to the Board, who then authorize the signing and sealing of the certificates; this is usually given effect by a resolution, which would appear in the minutes.

Where there is a large number of certificates to be signed and sealed, there will be no mention in the minutes as to who is to sign them, beyond the statement as to the numbers of directors who must attach their signatures thereto, and it is usual for the directors to arrange with the secretary as to the number that each will sign. In any case, it is well for the secretary to place his signature on the certificates after all details have been entered on them, but before they are signed and sealed by the directors. Meanwhile, a notice will be sent to all shareholders to the effect that on receipt of the allotment moneys and installment money, if any, the company will deliver them share certificates of title.

When the certificates are forwarded, a receipt should always be asked for, and, where possible, under the ordinary signature of the shareholder. Frequently shareholders require their certificates to be sent to their brokers or bankers, to some special address, and such cases can easily be acted on in the form of letters of advice.

On receipt of the letters of allotment, they should be scrutininized and then cancelled by writing or stamping by rubber stamp across the face of them the word "cancelled," and this is perhaps more effectual if the cancellation be shown on any signatures on the receipt, etc. When cancelled, they should be placed in numerical or alphabetical order and filed.

Loss of Document of Title

It occasionally happens that the shareholder will report that he has lost, mislaid or destroyed a share certificate, or temporary document of title such as on allotment letter.

In such circumstances a note of the loss should always be made on the member's account in the Register of Members, so that should the document later be presented, whether by some unauthorized person who is attempting to sell the shares, or by the member himself, the matter will receive prompt attention.

The member usually asks for a duplicate certificate to be issued on him, and the Articles of most companies authorize the directors to accede to such a request upon payment of a fee, and on such terms as to evidence of the loss and as to indemnity as they think fit. The directors may be satisfied with a letter of indemnity.

But most public companies require also a guarantee of the due observance of the undertaking, made by a bank or by persons of standing, together with a statutory declaration in which the member recites the facts under oath. The guarantee is frequently endorsed on the letter of indemnity.

The secretary will in due cause place these documents before the Board, and if they decide to issue a duplicate it will be marked "duplicate" before issue, and the fact of the issue will be noted on the member's account.

When Share Certificates are issued

In concluding it will be useful to set out the circumstances under which share certificates are issued

1. In exchange for letters of allotment and cash receipts.
2. In respect of a duly registered transfer.
3. In respect of a surrendered share warrant.
4. In respect of shares acquired by a person as a consequence of the death or bankruptcy of a member (after lodgment of written request to be registered as a member,

surrender of old certificates, and exhibition of probate, letters of administration, bankruptcy order, etc.).

5. On the marriage of a female shareholder (after production of a marriage certificate and surrender of share certificate in her previous name) though endorsement of the old certificate is usually sufficient.

6. In exchange for a worn out or defaced certificate, or in respect of one which has been lost, mislaid, destroyed or stolen.

7. In exchange for a certificate lodged to be split (i.e. where a certificate of a certain number of shares is surrendered and two more certificates are required, each for a part of shares).

8. In exchange for a balance receipt.

Stopple

A few words about what is known as the doctrine of estoppels should be given here. A company is stopped (i.e., precluded) from denying that the person named in the share certificate as the holder of a certain number of shares, is entitled to such shares. This is called estoppels as to title. Estoppels as to payment applies when a certificate states that the shares are paid for up to a certain amount. The company is stopped from denying that the amount stated has not actually been paid.

XIV

CALLS

WHERE a company is formed to purchase an existing business, it may require the whole amount of its capital within a short time of its formation to enable it to complete the purchase and provide the necessary cash and other liquid assets which form the working capital. In such circumstances the prospectus will probably provide that the whole price of shares will be payable by two or more installments within a few months of allotment, and will specify the amount of each installment and the date upon which it will be payable.

When, however, a company does not require all its capital until it has been operating for some time, a considerable proportion of the capital may be left to be called up in one or more "calls" as and when the money is required.

The Articles usually authorize the directors to make calls, and normal provision in the Articles is that no call shall exceed one-fourth of nominal amount of the share, and that it will not be payable at less than a period of one month from the last call, notice of fourteen days (or more) being given in respect of each call. Further stipulations often appearing in the Articles are that interest may be charged on the amount of calls where not paid on due dates and that calls may be paid in advance, interest being allowed thereon.

The resolution making a call will be passed at a Board meeting.

Following this resolution a call notice would be issued.

Before preparing the notice, all transfers accepted up to date of the call, i.e. the passing of the resolution would be passed by the Board and entered in the Register of Members.

Call lists are then prepared from the register, the names and addresses may first be inserted, and the sheets afterwards divided amongst clerks for the insertion of the number of shares against each name and the working out of the amounts due. Care must be taken to omit shareholders who have paid their calls in advance. Finally, the total of the "No. of shares" column is agreed with the total number of shares issued, and it is ascertained that the total amount called bears the correct proportion to the number of shares.

The call notices on which the names and addresses have been inserted by the addressing machine-are then filled in from the lists, checked and posted.

As members pay their calls, the payment
Will be entered on the lists. The secretary

Must be careful to see that transfer
received after the due date are declined

If the call has not been paid on the
shares therein.

There are interesting software programmes specifically to deal with records relating to calls.

XV
DIVIDENTS

DIVIDEND is a portion of the profit payable to the shareholders per share or per cent of the capital of the company.

Distributable Profits

As to what are profits available for dividend, that is a matter not capable of a ready answer, as much depends upon the circumstances attaching to each individual case. Certain general principles may, however, be lay down, though even not within the scope of the present book.

Profits available for dividend should be net profits from trading, and no dividend should be paid unless (with any credit balance brought forward from the previous year) there is a sufficient balance to the credit of Profits and Loss Accounts. Many companies, however, set aside a proportion of their profits in prosperous years to a "Dividend Equalization Reserve," and this reserve may be drawn upon in lean years. Legally, any reserve, accumulated out of profits, may be used for the payment of dividend, provided it has not been irrevocably capitalized, e.g. by the issue of bonus shares.

Finally, it is obvious that, whatever the state of the Profit and Loss Account, a cash dividend cannot be paid if the liquid resources of the company are thereby dangerously depleted.

The net profit is usually arrived at after charging all expenses, costs of trading, providing for depreciation and maintenance of plant, machinery, and other assets, including leases; for bad and doubts; for all amounts paid by way for interest and other items of a like character, some of which may be mentioned in the company's Articles. After such deductions have been made the directors will make whatever provision is considered necessary for reserve funds, such amounts to be employed either within or without the company's business. The amount then standing to the credit of Profit and Loss Account may be said to be "available for dividend." The amount which the directors propose to transfer to reserve and to distribute as dividend must be shown in the directors' report, which must accompany the annual accounts send to shareholders before the annual general meeting.

Organization of Dividend Payments

When the net profit available for dividend has been determined, the Articles should be examined to see who must participate in it. Where preference shareholders have cumulative rights in regards to dividends and have not in prior periods received the latter, their claims with respect thereto must first be satisfied. Unless the Articles provide otherwise, dividends are paid on the nominal amount of each share.

Most Articles provide that dividends other than interim dividends (which the directors may declare and pay when the profits justify) may only be declared by the company in general meeting; but that dividend shall not exceed the amount or rate recommended by the directors. The directors usually act on the assumption that their recommendation will be accepted and they have the dividend warrants prepared so that they may be dispatched immediately after the shareholders' meeting. The decisions of the directors will be embodied in resolutions;

   i.   To recommend that a certain rate of dividend be paid on a certain date, to persons appearing on the register on a specified date;
   ii. To close the register and transfer books, if that is the practice of the company;
   iii. To authorize the necessary dividend arrangements with the bank.

These resolutions will usually be passed alone with resolutions whereby the directors adopt the draft of the directors' report, authorize the distribution thereof with of the audited accounts, and convene the annual general meeting.

Notice of the closing of the register must be given by advertisement. Closing of the transfer books may be notified in the notice convening the meeting or be included in the advertisement.

All transfers received up to a fixed date or up to the date of closing the books, will be submitted to the Board and entered without delay in the Register. The shareholders' account will then be balanced, and the balance of each account inserted in the balance column.

The preparation of the Dividend List is then put in hand. A separate list may be prepared for those members who have lodged mandates requiring payment to be made to a bank; otherwise the list will be made out in the same sequence as the accounts appear in the register.

The names and addresses are inserted on the lists and the balanced shown in each members account is transferred to the list. This is then totaled and agreed with the number of shares known to be in issue, or with the total in each sectional register, as the case may be. The total amount represented in the "Tax" column should be equal to that at the current rate on the total sum. If there is any material variation in these, an error has been made. A difference of a small amount only may be due to fractions of a shilling being charged or deducted from the individual amounts. Whilst the Dividend List is being prepared the Dividend Warrants will have been printed and serially numbered.

Dividend Mandates

Many shareholders give instructions for their dividend to be paid to their bankers or brokers, and any such instructions must be carefully noted on the shareholder's account.

Where there is a large number of these dividends mandates, it is usual to send to the head office of each of the respective banks, one cheque of the total dividend payable to that bank, the cheque being accompanied by the upper halves if the warrants and a detailed list. The head office will distribute the upper halves to the appropriate branches of the bank, by which the dividends will be credited to the respective shareholders.

The work of dealing with such banks payments is facilitated if all accounts so affected are kept in a separate register (or one for each bank if sufficiently numerous).

Lost Dividend Warrants

Warrants are occasionally lost or destroyed, and an application made to the company for a duplicate. The secretary will, before placing such a request before the Board, ascertain all the facts, and further, will demand a letter of indemnity from the shareholder.

Interim Dividends

When the financial position of the company is such as to justify the payment of a dividend before the close of its financial year, such an interim dividend may be declared by the directors if the Articles give them the power to do so.

Interest on Shares

Brief mention may be made at this point of Sect. 67 of the companies Act, which allow interest to be paid on shares issued to meet the cost of constructing works or providing plan, and states that this interest may be charged at capital as part of the cost of constructing works or providing plant, and states that this interest may be charged to capital as part of the cost of construction of the work or building, or the provision of plant.

XVI
TRANSFER AND TRANSMISSION

In the previous chapter, reference was made to the fact that shares may pass from a holder by the process of forfeiture, but by such means only a very limited number shares pass from holder by what is known as "transfer," whilst a fair number pass by "transmission."

As mentioned earlier, transfer work in a company is usually undertaken by the company secretary, but if the transfers are numerous, there is often an officer responsible for the transfer work, known as the registrar, who for this purpose is immediately subordinate to the secretary, and the latter being always responsible to the board of directors for any share transactions in his company. Transfer work demands the greatest care in its execution.

Transfer of Shares

Transfer of shares occurs when, two parties having respectively agreed to part with and accept the legal title in shares, the name of the former is removed from the Register of Member in respect of such shares, and the name of the latter is inserted in his place.

The usual reason of transfer is simply that the shareholder has sold his shares; but shares also frequently change hands for the reasons given hereafter, whilst transfer may also take place as a result of a gift.

The Companies Act provides that, notwithstanding anything in the Articles of a company, it is not lawful to register a transfer of shares or debentures unless a proper instrument of transfer has been delivered.

The stock transfer form, signed by the transferor and stamped, is passed with the share certificate and forwards a returnable transfer receipt to the lodging agent or a broker. A new certificate is issued as quickly as possible and placed, together for approval. When approved, the new certificate is signed and sealed, and in due course finds its way onto the hands of the transferee. The Register of Members is amended to record the change in ownership of the shares.

The Stock Exchange

Sales of shares in public companies are more frequently arranged through the medium of stockbrokers and the Nairobi Stock Exchange. The member desiring to sell, instructs

His stockbroker to a price for his shares. The broker having obtained a price in the market concerned, the reports to his client and obtains his instructions to sell, and completes the deal.

Certification

The certification of transfers is procedure that takes place when, for example, a member of a company wishes to sell a part only, says one half, of his shareholding. He surrenders the share certificate to his broker who makes use of his provided by all stock exchanges and arranger for the transfer form, covering one half of the shares, to be "certified." What happens is that the stock exchange, having satisfied itself to the transaction, impresses its stamp to the transfer from which the broker certificate. For the "uncertified" balance of one half of the shares the register will issue a non-refundable balance ticket, and soon as possible prepare and dispatch a new certificate for the balance.

The legal effect of certification is that any person acting on the faith of a certification may assume that there have been produced to the Stock Exchange, and to the company, documents that establish the transferor's title to the shares or debentures named therein.

Passing the Transfer

Ever transfer lodged for registration must be covered by a surrendered certificate or other documents of title, and must be carefully scrutinized. The name of the company must be correctly stated; the distinctive number of shares must be checked; many companies compare the signature of the transferor which any previous signature available; any alteration must be initialed. Normally, an advice should be sent to the transfer, stating that unless his advices the contrary at once the transfer will be assumed in order. If the transfer has been certified, the notice will have been sent then.

Finally, the instrument must bear an impressed stamp for the correct amount. Briefly, this is at the rate of the consideration stated unless-

i.   The consideration is nominal one, when the duty is fixed, or
ii. The transfer is by way of gift, in which case it must usually bare the adjudication stamp and to be stamped at the ad valorem rate of market price of the shares.

The new certificates are prepared and checked, and are listed already to place before the board. At this stage many companies require their auditors to conduct an audit and to certify that all is in order. Otherwise it certifies against the transfer and to satisfy themselves that the old certificates have been cancelled. A resolution is then passed authorizing the signing, sealing and issue of the new certificates.

In due course the certificates are dispatched in accordance with the signed instructions of members entitled to them or are exchanged over the counter for Transfer Receipts and Balance Tickets. The Register of members is posted back to their counterfoils, and the Transfers are filed away. Some companies keep a Register or Transfers, but it is suggested that the ideal method is to file the completed transfers (with correspondence and old certificates attached) in date order, afterwards binding them in book form when they become sufficiently numerous. Binding in fifties and hundreds is found to be convenient.

Power of Attorney

Transfers may be executed by an agent under the authority of a power if attorney. The deed if appointment must be exhibited to the company for registration and it must be carefully examined to see what power is given to the holder. The authority delegated is interpreted strictly in accordance with written terms of the deed, and therefore it is particularly necessarily to assert whether the agent is authorized to buy shares sell shares, receive dividends, and to appoint substitutes.

Usually, they continue in force until revocation actually takes place, which may occur either by the definite act of the principal, i.e. cancellation, or upon his death, bankruptcy or unsoundness of mind. The secretary should before acting upon the power of attorney satisfy himself that it has not been revoked, and in some cases it may be desirable to require the attorney to execute a statutory declaration that the power is still in force.

The statement that the power of attorney has been exhibited, with brief particulars of the document, should be entered in the shareholder's account in the Register of members and in the Register of Power of Attorney.

Forged Transfers

A forged transfer (i.e. one in which the transferor's signature is a forgery) us a nullity and confers no right if title to the shares upon the transferee. Where the company has acted on such a transfer, the rightful owner can compel the company to restore his name to the register. If any dividends have, in the meantime, been paid to the alleged transferee, the company must also make good on those dividends to the true owner. The latter's remedy, in all cases, is against the company.

The Transferee, though he may have acted innocently, is a party to the nullity and loses his shares, and will be obliged to repay and dividends received.

If the company has issued a share certificate and a third party, relying on it has purchased the shares and suffered loess, the company (being unable to deny the declaration made in its certificate) will be reliable to compensate him. The company, provided it has taken very reasonable precautions has the right to recover the whole of

Its losses from the original transferee and his broker, both of whom, by asking the company to act on the transfer, impliedly warranted it to be genuine.

To meet payment made by the company in this matter, a reserve fund or compensation fund may be created, or the company may charge an additional fee to the usually one.

Few companies, however, take advantage of these acts; and most companies prefer to reply, first, upon precautions to avoid the registration of forged transfers; and, secondly, upon insurance to compensate them for any loss that might be incurred under forged transfers and forged power of attorney.

Restrictions of Transfers

Most Articles give the director of a company power to refuse to register a transferee of share. The Act should be referred to in that connections Private Companies must, of course, restrict transfer. Should the directors refuse to register a transfer, notice of refusal must be given to the transferee within two months of the lodgment of the transfer form.

Transmission

By "transmission" is meant the passing of the right to deal with share from one person to another by act or operation of law. Thus, in the case of deceased shareholder, the rights pass to the executors or administrators appointed to wind up the estate; in case of bankruptcy, to a trustee in bankruptcy, and where the shareholder is a person of unsound mind, the rights pass to his trustee.

The executors or administrators have the right to transfer the shares in their official capacity, but they may also, if they choose, request the company to place their names on the register, in which case they will be treated precisely in the same manner as other shareholders and will be responsible for liabilities attaching to the shares, likewise being entitled to any benefits there from. The company's Articles must consulted the ascertain whether a formal transfer is required.

A trustee should present his order to prove his appointment. It should be noted that a trustee in bankruptcy may, if he thinks fit, disclaim the shares of the bankrupt, as, for example, when there is a liability for unpaid calls.

As already mentioned, a Transfer Register is sometimes used in transfer work, and, for entry in the Register of Members; but the modern tendency is to dispense with this book and enter the particulars into the register of member direct from the transfer form.

XVII
FORFEITURE OF SHARES

THE Articles of most public companies give the directors power to forfeit shares, where installments or calls due thereon have not been paid after appropriate notice has been given to the shareholders of the directors' intention. There is no right to forfeiture unless it is given by the Articles; and where it exists it is essential that the directors should very carefully carry out procedure laid down, as in the event of any irregularity the dispossessed shareholders may be able to have the forfeiture annulled.

Forfeiture is, however, resorted to only when all efforts at persuasion have failed; and it is usual to send the shareholder at least two previous communications, the first merely reminding him of the overdue amount and that interest may be charged on it, and the second warning him that if non-payment continues the directors will regretfully have to consider the question of forfeiture.

As to forfeiture itself, the procedure provided by table A is typical; the following is a summary -

- If the call is unpaid at the due date, the directors may serve notice requiring payment of the call with interest.
- In the notice a date must be mentioned - no less than 14 days from the date of such notice - by which time the call must be paid, otherwise the shares are liable to forfeiture.
- On failure to comply with such notice, the directors may by resolution declare the shares forfeited.

- Forfeited shares may be disposed of as thought fit by the directors, or forfeiture may be cancelled.
- Persons whose shares are thereby forfeited, though ceasing membership of the company in respect of such shares, remain liable for all calls until payment of the nominal amount of shares is made in full.
- A statutory declaration, in writing, that the declaring is a director or secretary of the company and that a share in the company has been duly forfeited on a given date, is sufficient and conclusive evidence against all persons calming to be entitled to the shares. The person whom the share is disposed of shall be registered s holder. He is not bound to see to the application of purchased money nor is his title defective by irregularity of proceedings in reference to forfeiture.

To effect the forfeiture two board meetings are necessary, the first to give instructions for the formal notice to be issued (it should be sent by registered post); and the second after the date stated in the notice, to pass the resolution of forfeiture.

It is usual it send the shareholder to send notice to remove any suspicion he may have. It is also usual to request him to return the share certificate; but is rare for a defaulting member to comply with such request, and the result is that, should shares be sold and certificate issued to the purchaser, two documents of title will be on issue to the block shares. The Statutory declaration mention above is designed to nullify the validity of unreturned certificate.

Forfeited shares may be sold by the company at a discount not exceeding the amount paid to them at the time of sale.

Students sometimes inquire why, a person having acquired shares, wishes to disclaim them. The reason is that trading of a company proceeds it may become obvious that it will never prosper. Accordingly a shareholder may not wish to pay calls due, this being probably a matter of "throwing good money after bad." The Act that prevents such a person from evading liability.

Shares may be surrendered but only in cases where forfeiture would be valid; otherwise it would operate as a reduction of capital. A surrender can therefore, be in a respect of partly paid shares only.

THE COMMON SEAL

In the preceding pages some mention has been made of the seal and the sealing of documents. In the Companies Act there are the following among other references to it. "Every limited company shall have its name engraved in legible characters on its seal," and where a seal is used regardless of this regulation, the company and other officer of a limited company or any person acting on its behave using or authorizing the use of such seal and purporting it to seal of the company will each be liable to a penalty.

Contracts may in the same manner be varied and discharged. In practice the seal is used as the official signature of the company in important documents, e.g. share certificates, debentures, trust deeds, power of attorney. It is customary for the Articles to give directions as to sealing.

Directions are often made by the directors as to the custody of the seal. The usual rule is for it to be kept in a safe in the secretary's office, and in keys, usually two, are kept, one by the chairman or managing director or the other by secretary, duplicate keys being either held by other directors or deposited in a place of safety.

The sealing documents may be performed at Board Meetings and this procedure is followed where the documents are few in number. Where, however, large numbers of documents, e.g. share certificates, have to be sealed, it is usually found more convenient to pass, at the board meeting, a resolution authorizing the seal to be affixed to a certain directors to carry the resolution into effect.

XVIII

BORROWING POWERS-
DEBENTURES AND LOANS

FROM time to time many companies find it necessary to raise additional money in order to more effectually to carry out their business transactions, but instead of issuing further shares they often fine it more expedient to raise loans.

ALL trading companies, unless expressly forbidden to do so by their memorandum or Articles, have implied powers to borrow to any extent, and it may be noted that the power to borrow includes the power to give security; but it is usual to insert in the Articles provisions with regard to the maximum amount which the director may borrow as a temporary measure, as in the case of bank overdrafts and short loans granted by bankers and others for the advance of certain moneys or for credit during a heavy buying season, with or without security beyond that of the recognized "standing" of the permanent character, as required for something of a permanent character, as, for instance, to enable a company to have more working capital, or to erect buildings, the common practice is to issue a mortgage or debenture, given as security a charge upon the assets of the company.

Debentures

A debenture is understood to mean a security given by a company, under seal, to secure the repayment of borrowed money, with interest.

Debentures are of two kinds"

1. Simple.
2. Mortgage debentures.

Simple as the same implies gives on security; and a holder in a winding up would rank only as an ordinary creditor.

A mortgage debenture gives fixed or a floating charge or both. When a fixed charged is given, specific fixed assets, such as land, buildings, and plant, are charged and are conveyed at the lenders or trustees until repayment is effected; meanwhile the company has the use of the property, but cannot dispose of it or deal with it in any way without the consent of the debenture holder. A floating charge however, is a device intended to permit a company to borrow on the security of assets which are used in trading, such as stocks, work in progress, and book debt, which change from day to day consequently could not be charged in the manner indicated above. A floating charge permits the company to deal with assets charged in the ordinary course of business as if no charge existed until the charge "crystallized" or becomes fixed; this happens when the company is wound up, or default is made by the company on carrying out the terms of the loan and debenture holders or their trustees takes steps to enforce their security.

Frequently a debenture gives a fixed charge over certain fixed property which it specifies, and a floating charge over all the assets of the company, including its undertaking and its circulating assets, and its uncalled capital.

Trust deed

Where a debenture is issued to secure a single loan, such a bank overdraft, the debenture itself will contain the charge; but it is usually necessary to make use of a trust deed. This is a contract executed by the company and by trustees acting on behalf of the debenture holders; it has of necessity to be executed before the debenture are offered for subscription. It is very necessary that the company, in arranging for trustees, should either invite two or three men oh high standing in commerce-whose name will inspire the confidence of investors-to act, or appoint to the duty one or other of the "trustee" companies formed to undertake such work.

The trust deed states that maximum amount of the issue, the rate of interest and when payable, and the date and terms of redemption; it provides that the trustee shall hold the title deeds of the property subject to a fixed charge, and requires the company to keep the property insured and in repair; and entitles the trustees, in any defaults is made, to appoint a receiver a receiver or take other steps to enforce the security. It may also provide for meetings with debenture holders and for a resolution passed for meetings with debentures holders and for a resolution passed by a specified majority at such a meeting to bind all debenture holders. The benefit of the deed is given to every debenture holder. The benefit of the deed is given to every debenture holder for reference in the debenture or stock certificate as the case may be.

It should be noted that any provision contained in a trust deed is void if it has the effect of exempting a trustee from breach of trust where he fails to show due care and diligence.

Forms of Debentures

The following forms of debenture are issued by limited companies-

Debentures to bearers, with or without interest coupons attached.

Debentures to registered holders.

Debentures stock.

Debenture stock is loan capital consolidated. A lender will thus have certificate entitling him to a certain amount or stock in accordance with the amount he advances.

In the case of an issue of debenture to registered holder, each debenture certificate or bond is usually a specific mortgage for a fixed amount named therein, and bares its own stamp duty, but a trust deed may also be made for such debentures.

Issue of Debentures

When a company desire to issue debentures, the directors will pass a resolution authorizing their creation. Such resolution may be the following terms, but, in as much as the company's lawyers would be engaged in the preparation of the debentures, and perhaps of the trust deed, the actually form of resolution would be drafted by them.

The methods adopted in issuing debentures follow very closely those used in issuing shares. Underwriting arrangements are made and a prospectus issued. In this connection it should be noted that, although a company may not exercise any borrowing powers (this would include allotting debentures) until it is entitled to commence business, Sect. 11, of the Companies Act, Cap 486, provides that it may before that date issue a prospectus and offer shares and debenture simultaneously, and receive application money therefore.

Not return of allotments is necessary for debenture issue.

Scrip Certificate

Debentures are usually paid up by installment over few months of allotment. It will be appreciated that the actual debenture or stock certificates cannot be issued until payment in full had been made, and it usual, therefore, to issue script certificates. These are made out to bearer, and provided receipt forms on which the company's bankers can record payment of installment. When all installments have been paid, the holder is entitled, on filling in his name and address, to exchange the scrip for the actual debenture or dividend debenture stock certificate, made out in his favor. The transfer of script certificate is merely by passing hand to hand. No stamp duty is payable.

Registration of Debenture

When the bonds have been prepared, they must be registered in accordance with Sect. 96 of the Companies Act, and this must be done within twenty-one days of the creation of the mortgage or charge on the company's assets to which each refers. The section referred to should be carefully studied by the secretary. Failure to register may cause the charge to become invalid against a liquidator or creditor, and the money to become immediately repayable. The Registrar issues a certificate on the registration of any mortgage or charge, stating the amount secured, and copy of this certificate must be endorsed on every debenture or certificate of debenture stock issued by the company in

Respect of which the payment is secured by the mortgage or charge registered. In practice, this copy certificate is put on the debenture certificate by a rubber stamp.

In manner similar to that adopted in the case of an issue of shares, the applicants for debenture are requested to toward their receipts to be exchanged for debenture bonds. Delivery of such bonds should either be affected personally or by registered post, and an acknowledgement of their safe receipt asked for in every case. As in the case of shares, debenture bonds or certificates must be ready for issue within two months after allotment has been made, unless the conditions of issue otherwise provide.

Register of charges must be kept by every company, in which must be recorded all charges specifically affecting the property of the company of the company and all floating charges on the undertaking or any property of the company, giving in each case a short description of the property charged, the amount of the charge and (except in the case of securities to bearer) the names of the persons entitled thereto. Any creditor or member of a company, may, inspect the Register of Charges and copies of the instruments making or creating the charges at reasonable times. The Register of Charges is also open to the inspection of any other person on payment of a free for each inspection. If the provisions governing the issue of the debentures require that a Register of Debenture Holders be kept (which is usual, as otherwise payment of interest by the company's staff would be seriously hampered), it must be kept at the company's registered office or at any other place where it is made up. The Register of Debenture Holders is open to inspection of any holder of such debentures and of any holders of shares in the company without free. The Act requires a company to keep at its registered office a copy of all mortgages to keep at its registered office a copy of all mortgage and charges which have to be registered.

If inspection of these registers and documents is refused, the company and every officer of the company in default are liable to a fine, and further to a default fine. The Court may be order to compel an immediate inspection of the register or director that the copies required shall not be sent to the person requiring them.

The Companies Act, allows the Register of Debenture Holders to be kept either at the registered office of the company or at any other office at which that work of making it up is done.

Transfer of Debenture

Though transfer of registered debenture is almost the same as that of shares, the new stock transfer from being almost always used, it is pointed out that new debenture bonds are not issued after transfer, but the bones is endorsed.

In transfer of debenture stock the old certificate is cancelled and a new certificate is sealed and issued.

Barer debentures pass by delivery and, like share warrants are negotiable instruments.

Redemption

The date of the redemption is generally stated on the debenture bond or certificate, and a reference is frequently inserted therein to the effect that such bond can, at the option of the company, be redeemed at a prior date. Notice of redemption is usually given by public advertisement in a newspaper and by circular to debenture holders, standing the time, place and payment. A receipt is obtained, on the debenture being redeemed, the secretary will complete a form, and on the receipt of this, the Registrar will grant a Memorandum of Satisfaction, a copy of which should be entered on Register of Debentures. He certificates or bonds will be cancelled and securely filed away.

Re-issue of Debenture

Debenture mat be re-issued. The Companies Act deals with this matter.

"Where either before or after the commencement of this Act, a company has redeemed any debentures previously issued, then:-

a) Unless any provision of the contrary, whether expressed or implied, is contained in the Articles or in any contract entered in to by the company; or
b) Unless the company has, by passing a resolution to that effect or by some other act, manifested its intention that the debenture shall be cancelled;

The company shall have, and shall be deemed always to have has, power to re-issue the debenture, either by re-issuing the same debentures or by issuing other debentures in their place."

Sect. 92 (2) enacts that one a re-issue the person entitled to the debenture shall have the same priorities as if the debenture has never been redeemed.

It is to be observed, however, that, for purposes of stamp duty; re-issued debentures must be treated as new debentures and, accordingly, must be re-stamped upon re-issue.

Where a company has power to re-issue debenture which have been redeemed, particulars with respect to the debentures must be included in every Balance Sheet or the company.

A Memorandum of Satisfaction should not be filed in respect of debentures which have been redeemed and which are intended to be available for re-issue.

XIX

INCREASE AND REDUCTION OF CAPITAL

SOMETIMES it is found necessary to alter the company's original capital, and the Articles of Association should be so framed as to give the necessary powers, which must, of course, be within the provisions of the Companies Act. The alterations that may be under the Act are;

a) Increase of capital

b) Consolidation, decision and subdivision of the share capital,

c) Conversion of paid up shares into stock, and reconversion of stock into paid up shares,

d) Redemption of redeemable preference shares,

e) Reorganization of capital,

f) Reduction or cancellation of capital.

Increase

An increase of capital is often required by a company having an expanding business, and where the amount of registered capital has been issued; recourse must be had to loan capital or to the issue of shares above the maximum allowed by the Memorandum of Association. A company limited by shares may alter the conditions of its Memorandum, if so authorized by its Article, that it may increase its share capital by issue of a new shares of such amount as it thinks expedient. The power must be exercised by the company in general meeting. Notice of the increase must be given to the Registrar of Companies within fifteen days after the date of the passing of the resolution; this is accompanied by a printed copy of the resolution, authorizing the increase. The notice must include the prescribed particulars of the classes of shares affected by the increase of capital, which attracts stamp duty. If default made in complying with this section, the company and every officer who is in default are liable to a default fine.

The Articles usually stipulate that in respect of further issues of shares, the existing holders shall have a right to a prior offer of the new shares in proportion to their holding.

Reduction

The companies Act require that, a company if so authorized by its Article may in general meeting cancel shares which, at the date of the passing of the resolution, have not been taken or agreed to be taken by any person, and diminish the amount of shares capital by the amount of the shares so cancelled; but a cancellation of shares in this way is not deemed to be a reduction of shares capital within the meaning of the Act.

A company limited by shares reduces its capital usually for one of the following reasons:-

1. It has more capital than it can profitably employ in the business; or
2. Some of its capital has been lost or is unrepresented by available assets.

In the latter case the profit-earning power of the company is usually much reduced, so that the dividends which can be paid are very low when reckoned as a percentage. The remedy is to reduce the capital to such an amount as represent the real value, the revenue-earning point of view, of the remaining assets.

Where the preference shares rank in priority as regards capital, the ordinary shares must first be written down, but in many cases a compromise is affected and both preference and ordinary shareholders bear some part of the lost. The ordinary shareholders, however, must obviously bear the greater portion.

The Act gives the following methods of reducing capital –

1. By extinguishing or reducing the liability or any shares of the company in respect of shares capital not paid up.
2. By cancelling any paid up share capital which is lost or underrepresented by available assets, either with or without extinguishing or reducing liability on its shares.

3. By paying off any paid up shares capital which is in excess of the wants of the company, either with or without extinguishing or reducing liability on any of its shares.

To effect a reducing of capital, a special resolution must first be passed by the company, and after the passing of this, application may be made to the Court for an order conforming the reduction. Where the reduction involves a diminution of liability in respect of unpaid share capital or the payment to any shareholders of any paid up share capital, creditor are entitled to object and all objections creditors must be paid off or must be secured in terms of Sect. 69 (2) of the Act. Where, however, the reductions does not involve the diminution of any liability in respect of unpaid capital or the payment to the shareholders of any unpaid up capital,

Creditors are not entitled to object, nor, unless the Court requires it, is their consent necessary. The court may make an order confirming the reduction on such terms as it thinks fit, and May –

a) Make an order that the company must add to its name for a specified period in words "and reduced"; and

b) Make an order requiring publication of reduction or such other information in regard thereto as the Court may think expedient with a view to giving proper information to the public.

When the Court has made an order sanctioning the reduction, a copy of this, together with a minute showing full details on the new share capital, must be filled with the registrar, who will them forward a certificate to the company. This is convulsive evidence that the terms of the Companies Act have been compiled with. The share certificates must be called in and rectified accordingly, and the necessary alterations made in the Register of Members. Where the shares are reduced in nominal value, the fact will be indicated by a memorandum across the face of the certificate and at the head of each folio of the register – a rubber stamp giving the particulars will suffice.

It is perhaps needless to add that reduction of capital should not be undertaken without legal advice.

XX

OTHER CHANGES IN SHARE CAPITAL

A COMPANY may, if authorized by its Articles, alter its capital by:-

1. Increasing its authorized capital;
2. Converting fully paid shares into stocks;
3. Re-converting stock into fully paid shares;
4. Consolidating its shares into shares of a larger amount;
5. Cancelling unissued capital;
6. Reducing its capital;
7. Redeeming redeemable preference shares.

The Companies Act provide that where authority is granted by the Articles a company limited by shares may convert all or any of its paid up shares into stock, and re-convert that stock into paid up shares of any general meeting. An ordinary resolution is sufficient unless the Articles stipulations otherwise. Where no provision is made in the Articles for conversion of shares into stock, the Articles would have to be altered by special resolution to allow for it.

Stock represents fully paid capital, and can only be created by conversion; it cannot be issued in the first place. Theoretically it may be transferred in any amount, however small; but in practice that Articles almost always provide that it may be transferred only multiples.

The Companies Act provides that all the issued shares in a company, or all issued shares of a particular class are fully paid-up and rank **pair pass** for all purposes, it is unnecessary for them it have distinguishing numbers.

Particulars as regards stock issued and the holders of it must kept in manner similar to that required in the Register of Members for shares, and that ruling for the shares register will suffice, with the omission of the columns for distinctive numbers. When the resolution authorizing the conversation of fully paid shares into stock has been passed (which resolution may state the minimum amount of stocks that may be transferred, the books will be closed and the shares certificates called in and cancelled, and a schedule of shareholders and their holdings, on which to record the return of share holdings, on which to record the return of share certificates and the issue of stock certificates, will be prepared, the addressing machine being used to insert the names and addresses.

In making out this list, care must be taken to see that all transfers have been made and that the register is in perfect order. The stock share certificates, which are practically

The same as made for distinctive numbers, are then prepared, sealed, signed by the directors, and delivered in the manner as provided for shares.

If it is at any time desired, stock may be reconverted into shares subject to the same condition as to authority in the Articles, alteration of the Memorandum, and notifying the Registrar, as apply to the conversion of shares into stock. In this process, new distinctive numbers would be given to the shares issued on the reconversion (if necessary) instead of an old number being used. A new share register would be written up on the occasion of the reconversion.

Other Alteration of Capital

Sect. 63 of the Companies Act also empowers a company limited by shares or a company limited by guarantee and having a share capital, where its Article authorize it, to:-

a) Consolidate and divide all or any of its shares capital into shares of larger amount then its existing shares; and

b) Subdivide its shares, or any of them into shares of smaller amount then is fixed by the Memorandum, so, however, that in the subdivision, the proportion between the amount paid and the amount, if any, unpaid on each reduced share shall be the same as it was the case of the share from which the reduced share is derived.

These powers must be exercised by the company in general meeting. Frequently the Memorandum or the Articles provide that such a reorganization may be effected by a resolution passed by or an agreement signed by particular majority of the class concerned. Where such a resolution is passed or agreement signed, a dissentient minority, if they hold not less than 15 per cent of the issued shares of the class, may the proposed variation of rights is then inoperative unless and until the court sanctions it.

Where the Memorandum or Articles do not make any provisions for the modification of the class rights, recourse can be had to a "compromise or arrangement" between the company and the classes of members concerned as provided under Sect. 207. Briefly, the procedure is to apply to the Court for an order that meetings of the various classes of shareholders shall be held. At these meetings the scheme will be proposed, and if a majority in number representing three-fourths in value of the members present and voting (either in person or by proxy) agrees to the scheme, it will, if sanctioned by the Court, be binding on the members and the company. The order of the Court sanctioning

The scheme must be filled with the Registrar, and a copy annexed to every copy of the Memorandum afterwards issued.

Notice of any such conversion, consolidation, division etc. must be given to the Registrar within one month, otherwise the company and its defaulting officers are liable to a default fine.

Every copy of the Memorandum of Association issued after he alteration must be in accordance therewith.

The Act prescribes for an ordinary resolution. Notice of the cancellation must be filled within one month.

Redeemable Preference Shares

Mention of these has been made previously, but the present chapter seems the most convenient one in which to give them special consideration. Sect. 60 of the Act gives accompany limited shares powers, if so authorized by its Articles, to issue preference shares which are, or at the option of the company are to be liable, to be redeemed. Where such shares have been issued, the following provisions apply:-

1. The shares may be redeemed only out of profits available for dividends or out of the proceeds of a fresh issue of shares made expressly for the purpose of redemption.
2. The shares to be redeemed must be fully paid up.
3. If the shares are redeemed out of profits, the company must transfer out of profits to a Capital Redemption Reserve Fund a sum equal to the nominal amount of the shares redeemed.

4. Any premium payable on redemption must be provided for out of profits, or out of the Share Premium Account, before the shares are redeemed.

5. Subject to the above, the redemption may be effected on such terms an in such manners as the Article of Association may provide.

6. The balance Sheet must show the part of the issued capital which consists of redeemable preference shares and the date of redemption.

7. The capital is not deemed to be increased for stamp duty purposes when shares up to the nominal amount of those redeemed or to be redeemed are issued, but the old shares must be redeemed within one month of the issue of the new one.

8. The Capital Redemption Reserve Fund may be applied in paying up unissued shares to be issued to members as fully paid bonus shares.

9. The redemption of preference shares under Sect. 58 is not to be taken as reducing the company's authorized share capital.

10. Notice of the redemption must be filled within one month.

Bonus Shares

A prosperous company that has pursued a conservative policy in the distribution of its profits may find itself, of course of time, with a large reserve of undistributed profits; frequently these profits are invested in the business and are therefore represented by assets such as plant and stocks, etc., and not by cash, and consequently the company is unable to distribute the accumulated profits by way of dividends. In such circumstance the Directors frequently decide to capitalize the profits, i.e. they use them, by means of a book entry, to pay up new shares, which are then issued to the shareholders in accordance with the dividend rights of the classes and in proportion to the holdings of the members. There otherwise than in cash, and must also authorize the capitalization of profits.

The allotment procedure takes the usual course, except that no applicants are required; and the allotment latter usually carry renunciation rights, to enable members to realize their bonus in cash by selling, if they so prefer. As fractions of share cannot be allotted, difficulties arising over such fractions in apportioning the bonus may be met by ignoring the fractions or by giving cash instead of fraction or by issuing fractional certificates for temporary use by shareholders until others have been collected to make up a whole number. Such fractional certificates give no right or membership.

The Nairobi Stock Exchange must be informed where applicable.

XXI

COMPANY BOOKS AND ACCOUNTS

Every company must keep proper books of account with respect to

a) Sums of money received and expanded by the company and the matters in respect of which the receipt and expenditure take place;

b) Sales and purchases of goods by the company;

c) Assets and liabilities of the company sect. 147, Companies act cap 486. In addition, limited companies are required to keep the following:-

1. Minute book
2. Register of members
3. Register of charges
4. Register of Directors and secretaries
5. Register of directors shareholders

And the following, among others are kept as required

6. Directors attendance book
7. Registrar of transfers
8. Register of important documents
9. Seal book
10. Share certificate book
11. Agenda book
12. Register of share warrants
13. Certification of transfers registered

14. Balance ticket(receipt) book
15. Register of debenture Holders
16. Register of probates, etc.
17. Register of powers of attorney
18. Separate transfer books or registers for recording transfers of debentures

Accounts

It is incumbent on all limited companies to keep accounts of their business transactions as mentioned in the beginning of this chapter. Sect 147 of the companies act stipulates that the book of account must be such as to give a true and fair view of the state of the company's affairs and explain its transactions by sect 147(2) of and to explain its transactions and financial positions and contain entries of the daily receipts and payments of cash and where goods are dealt in they must contain statements of annual stock takings, and except in the case of goods sold by way of ordinary retail trade off all goods sold and purchased showing the goods and they buyers and sellers thereof. A profit and loss account must be laid before the company in general meeting not later than eighteen months after the incorporation of the company and subsequently in every calendar year. Details of the particular to be shown in the profit and loss account.

Balance Sheet

The act also sets out the particulars to be given in a balance sheet which must give a true and fair view of the state of affairs at the end of the financial year.

Act sets out special provisions for a company which is either a holding or a subsidiary company requiring that the assets which represent shares in a subsidiary company must be set out separately in the balance sheet and profit and loss account.

The sets out special provisions for a company which is either a holding or a subsidiary company, requiring that the assets which represent shares in a subsidiary company must be set out separately in the balance sheet and that amounts owing to and from a subsidiary must be distinguished from all other liabilities and assets.

The companies act requires a company which has subsidiaries to lie before its members in general meeting with its own balance sheet and profit and loss account, accounts dealing with the state of affairs and profit and loss of the company and subsidiaries which are known as group accounts are set out in sects. 151 and 152 of the companies act further explanations regarding a financial year of a holding and a subsidiary company and the exact meaning of holding and a subsidiary are given then act.

The accounts which are to be put before general meeting annually must contain particulars as to the loans if any made to the directors and as to the director's remuneration.

The balance sheet must be accompanied by a report of the directors and state the amount if any recommended for divined and state the amount, if any which it is proposed to place to a reserve fund. It must be signed on behalf of the board by two directors or if there is only one director than by that director. The auditor's report on the accounts must be attached to the balance sheet and read at the annual general meeting.

If any copy of a balance sheet which has not been signed above is issued circulated or published or is so issued etc. without having attached a copy of the auditor's report attached or without have attached a copy of the profit and loss account, or any group accounts in a case of a holding company a penalty attaches to the company and to every officer of the company who is knowingly a party to the default.

The foregoing indicates the importance of constant reference to the Act.

The Secretary's Duties

Some general remarks may now be made on the accounts or statements of account with which the secretary has to deal.

These may be placed under two heads viz. the general accounts of the business and statements referring to accounts statistics etc. usually placed before directors for their consideration.

The secretary usually a competent account will be able to organize the book keeping and accounts if his company in such a manner as to exhibit at all times and without difficulty and delay the real position of affairs of the company. This is a matter in which he will be guided by the particular requirements of his directors and of the business. Where there is an official on the staff recognized as accountant much responsibility will be taken of the shoulders of the secretary but nevertheless he should be kneel alive to any possible improvements in the system, so as to ensure the fullest efficiency and dispatch. It may be the end often is desirable to confer with the auditors of the company when any departure is suggested in connection with the methods of any section of account keeping and frequently the auditors make recommendations in the matter. Whilst the principles of book- keeping are applied generally to all business in practice details very considerably and this is only natural, viewing the varying requirements of different companies. The alert secretary will therefore make himself cognizant with the details of his company's business and found his system in accordance with its needs

XXII

GENERAL DUTIES OF AUDITORS

Generally the duties of the auditors are to see that the assets bare actually in existence and the documents of title are in the possession of the proper parties that the valuation of such assets has appearanently been made on proper basis that all liabilities both actual and contingent are disclosed that a clear distinction has been made between capital and revenue; and the profit stated to been earned as actually been earned and that the accounts reflect the true financial position and are in accordance with any agreements articles of association or statutory requirements which govern their form or the transactions which such accounts record.

The auditors must report on every balance sheet every profit and loss account and all group accounts laid before the company in general meeting.

The duties of the auditors are not confined to the examination of the financial books only. The auditors do a limited company must examine the memorandum and articles of association the prospectus if any the purchase agreement of the minute book and the register of members and register of charges and they also usually audit the transfer register. Where a company has been incorporated by special act of parliament that act must eb examined by the auditors.

By law the auditors of companies incorporated under the companies act required to:

1. Verify the final accounts and report to the shareholders on the balance sheet profit and loss account and group accounts stating.
   a) Whether or not they have obtained all the information and explanations necessary for the audit;

b) Weather in their opinion proper books of account have been kept and proper returns have been received from branches not visited by them;

c) Whether the company's balance sheet and unless it is framed as a consolidated profit and loss account profit and loss account are in agreements with the books of accounts and returns;

d) Whether the accounts give the information required by the act in the manners required and give a true and fair view of the company's affairs and profit or loss of the company and subsidiaries.

Share Audits

In many companies the auditors check every transger and certificate before submission to the Board. They examine the stamp duty and while not verifying the signature of the transfer the secretary should do this should ask to see a copy of the power of attorney if a transfer is signed by an attorney if a transfer is signed by the executor or administrator or a deceased person of unsound mind or a trustee in bankruptcy the certificates should be closely scrutinized and if necessary reference should be made to the company's register of deeds. The register of members should be inspected from time to time I order to verify that the shareholding of each director has not fallen below the number stipulated as his minimum qualification.

The Appointment of auditors

limited companies must have an auditor or auditors appointed in conformity companies act. The first auditors are usually appointed and their remuneration fxed by the directors before the statutory meeting and they hold office until the conclusion of the first annual general meeting. Thenceforward the auditors are appointed or reappointed or a unless they are not qualified for reappointment or a resolution has been passed to the countrary or the auditors have given notice in writing of their unwillingness to be reappointed. The general practice is for auditors to be automatically reappointed without any resolution the standard entry on the agenda of the annual general meeting being to fix the remuneration of the auditors in the case of a casual vacancy the directors may fill it where there is a surviving auditor he continues to act.

No director or other officer may act as an auditor to the company no person who is a partner of or in the employ of any officer of a company is qualified for appointment as auditor of such company.

No person other than the retiring auditor may be appointed at an annual general meeting unless special notice of the resolution appointing another person is given in accordance with sect. 160 of the companies act cap 486. On receipt of such notice the company must forthwith send a copy to the retiring auditor.

Auditors have the right of access to the companys books and accounts and vouchers and have the right to attend and receive notices of and other communications relating to any general meeting they are also permitted to make any statement or explanation that they desire with respect to the accounts.

The remuneration of the auditors must be fixed at a general meeting of the company except in the case of any auditor appointed before the first annual general meeting or of an auditor appointed to fill a casual vacancy when it may be fixed by the directors if the remuneration of the auditors is not fixed by the company in general meeting the amount must be shown under a separate heading in the profit and loss account shareholders sometimes delegate to directors the power of fixing the amount of the auditors fees.

XXIII

ANNUAL RETURN

THIS can best be explained by reference to the particulars contained in sect. 125 and of the companies act and a copy of the official document which has to be filled up and placed in the hands of the Registrar of Companies.

The following is the substance of the provisions:

1. Every company having a share capital shall once at least in every year make a return congaing a list of all person who on the fourteenth day after the annual general meeting in the year are members of the company and of persons who have ceased to be members since the date of the last return or in the case of the first return of the incorporation of the company.

2. The list must state the names and addresses of each of the existing members and the number of shares held by each of the existing members at the date of the return specifying shares transferred since the date of the last return or in the case of the first return of the incorporation of the company by persons who are still members respectively and have ceased to be members respectively and the dates of registration of the transfers and if the names are not in alphabetical order must have annexed to it an index sufficient to enable any name in the list to be readily found.

3. The return must also state the address of the registered office of the company and musty contain a summary distinguishing between shares issued for cash and shares issued as fully or partly paid up otherwise than in cash and specifying the following particulars:

    a) The amount of the share capital of the company and the number of the shares into which it is divided.

b) The number of shares of each class taken up to the date of return;

c) The amount called up on each share

d) The total amount of calls received

e) The total amount of calls unpaid

f) The total amount of the same if any paid by way of commission in respect of any shares or debentures.

g) Particulars of the discount allowed on the issued at a discount or of so much as has not been written of

h) The total amount of the sums if any allowed by way of discount in respect of any debentures since the date of the last return

i) The total number of shares forfeited

j) The total amount of shares for which share warrants are outstanding

k) The total amount of share warrants issued and surrendered respectively since the date of the last return

l) The number of shares comprised in each share warrant

m) All such particulars with respect to the persons who at the date of the return are the directors of the company and any person who is secretary as are by this act required to be contained with respect to directors and the secretaries.

n) Particulars of the total amount of the indebtedness of the company in respect of all mortgages and charges which are required to be registered with registrar of companies

4. The return shall be in the form set out in the act or as near thereto as circumstances admit.

In any year if the return for either f the two immediately preceding years has given the full particulars of the members then the return need gave only particulars relating to persons ceasing to be or becoming members since the date of the last return and to shares transferred since that date or to changes as compared with the date in the amount of stock held by a member. This exception and others are set out the companies act on the other hand if a company fails to comply with the requirements of that section the company and every officer in default are liable to a default fine.

Sect. 126 provides for the completing provides and filling of the return within forty two days after the annual general meeting and states that it must be signed by both a director and a secretary of the company.

Private Companies

The act provides that every private company shall spend with the annual return a certificate signed both by a director and a secretary that the company has not since the date if the last return or in case of first return since incorporation issued any invitation to the public to subscribe for its shares or debentures and that where the total number of members exceeds fifty and that excess consists wholly of persons who, under paragraph the act, are to be excluded in reckoning the number of fifty.

COMET COMMERCIAL SERVICES

COMPANY SECRETARIAL QUESTIONAIRE FOR
PRIVATE LIMITED COMPANIES

PART A

1. NAME OF COMPANY:

2. COMPANY NUMBER: JURISDICTION:

3. REGISTERED OFFICE ADDRES:

4. DIRECTORS

    1. (MANAGING DIRECTOR)
    2.
    3.
    4.
    5.
    6.

5. COMPANY SECRETARY:

6. VAT NUMBER:

7. DORMANT? (Y/N)
   LAST SHARE CERT:

8. PRINCIPLE BUSINESS ACTIVITIES

9. AUDITORS:

10. TEL NO.:
    FAX NO.:

11. BANKERS – (1) NAME:
                  ADDRESS:
                  TEL NO.:
                  E.
            (2) NAME:
                  ADDRESS:
                  TEL. NO.:
                  FAX NO.:

12. DATE OF INCORPORATION: / / /

13. DATE OF ANNUAL RETURN: / / /

14. LAST ANNUAL RETURN (a) DATED: / / /
                        (b) FILED: / / /

15. DATE OF LAST AGM: / / /

16. a. DATE OF NEXT AGM: / / /
    b. MONTHS WARNING (AGM): YES/NO

17. a. START ACCOUNTING PERIOD: / / /
    b. END ACCOUNTING PERIOD. / / /

18. ACCOUNTS LAST FILED: / / /

19. PERIOD END LAST FILES ACCOUNTS: / / /

20. a. FILE NEXT ACCOUNTS: / / /
    b. ACCOUNTS: MONTHS WARNING: YES/NO

21. START NEXT AUDIT: / / /

PART B

ARTICLES

RETIREMENT OF DIRECTORS BY ROTATION: YES/NO (TABLE A #89)

PROPORTION OF DIRECTORS ROTATING: (NOT EXCEEDING) (TABLE A #89)

RE: ELECT DIRECTORS: YES/NO (TABLE A #91)

SHAREHOLDING QUALIFICATION: YES/NO (TABLE A #77)

PRE-EMPTION RIGHTS – ALLOTMENTS: YES/NO (ARTICLES)

PRE-EMPTION RIGHTS – TRANSFERS: (ARTICLES)

MAXIMUM DIRECTORS (NO): (TABLE A #74)

MINIMUM DIRECTOR (NO): (S 33 & TABLE A #74)

NORMAL RETIREMENT AGE: (ARTICLES)

CHAIRMANS VOTE OF BOARD MEETING: CASTING? YES/NO (TABLE A #98)

QUORUM AT BOARD MEETING: (NO.) (TABLE A #99)

CHAIRMANS VOTE AT GENERAL MEETING: CASTING YES/NO (TABLE A # 60)

QUORUM AT GENERAL MEETING (NO): (TABLE A #53)

SHORT NOTICE PERCENTAGE: S133

DATE (SHORT NOTICE PERCENTAGE): / / /